# The Promise Keepers

# The Promise Keepers

## *Politics and Promises*

Bryan W. Brickner

LEXINGTON BOOKS
*Lanham • Boulder • New York • Oxford*

LEXINGTON BOOKS

Published in the United States of America
by Lexington Books
4720 Boston Way, Lanham, Maryland 20706

12 Hid's Copse Road
Cumnor Hill, Oxford OX2 9JJ, England



British Library Cataloguing in Publication Information Available

**Library of Congress Cataloging-in-Publication Data**

Brickner, Bryan W., 1964-
The Promise Keepers : politics and promises / Bryan W. Brickner.
p. cm.
Includes bibliographical references and index.
ISBN 0-7391-0008-4 (alk. paper). – ISBN 0-7391-0059-9 (pbk. : alk. paper)
1. Promise Keepers (Organization) I. Title.
BV960.B75 1999
267'.23—dc21

99-10349
CIP

Printed in the United States of America

™ The paper used in this publication meets the minimum requirements of American National Standard for Information Sciences—Permanence of Paper for Printed Library Materials, ANSI Z39.48–1992.

*to Dianna,*
*thanks for loving me*

# Contents

# Preface

In Catholicism, the Preface is a thanksgiving prayer used to introduce the canon of the Roman Catholic Mass. It is a beginning to the pathway of piety. It introduces one to the ways of God.

This preface is not an introduction to a canon, it does not take the form of a prayer, and how (or if) one proceeds toward God is not of my concern. What this preface does is to invite. What follows is an invitation in thought. There is nothing one has to understand about the subject at hand, and, therefore, one is unencumbered by the quest for answers. What follows is a study on the Promise Keepers – an investigation, a discourse, and even a story.

It is not a polemic against the Promise Keepers, nor is it apologetic. If you read on you will find that there are many values and beliefs I admire about the men involved in Promise Keepers and in the movement in general. You will also find that there are many values and beliefs that I do not accept. It has not been my intention to delineate between the good and the bad; that is up to you.

Ah, but some of you have learned not to trust the author. Very well. A good lesson learned. I do not pretend to offer you complete objectivity. I have only tried to be honest to myself, my perceptions, and the men who shared their world with me.

I invite you to read on and decide for yourself.

# Acknowledgments

I wish to acknowledge and thank the faculty, staff, and friends at Purdue University for their support and efforts in this project. A special thanks to Mike Weinstein for his time and friendship.

I want to acknowledge the Changing Men Collections at Michigan State University for supplying an invaluable resource on the Promise Keepers.

Permission to reprint has been granted from: *Double Bind* by Rodney Cooper, copyright 1996 by Rod Cooper, used by permission of Zondervan Publishing House; *From Ashes to Glory* by Bill McCartney, with Dave Diles, copyright 1995, used by permission of Thomas Nelson, Inc., Publishers; *What Makes A Man?* by Bill McCartney, copyright 1992, used by permission of NavPress Publishing Group; "Building an Evangelical Organization: The Lincoln Bedroom or Oval Office Model?" by Bryan W. Brickner, in *Good News, or Dupes and Reactionaries?: The Promise Keepers*, edited by Dane Claussen, forthcoming, permission granted by Dane Claussen and McFarland & Company, Publishers; "The Promise Keepers as Social Capitalists," by Bryan W. Brickner, in *Social Structures, Social Capital, and Personal Freedom*, edited by Dale McConkey and Peter Lawler, forthcoming, permission granted by Greenwood Publishing Group.

I also want to thank the men and women who helped me to understand the Promise Keepers. Without their testimonies none of what follows would have been possible.

I have not meant to express my thought but to help
you clarify what you yourself think. . . .
Bataille, *Theory of Religion*

# Introduction

The Promise Keepers is a mutation of the men's movement, a nondenominational Christian organization that combines biblical values with a men's support group. From a modest beginning in 1990 of 70 men joining together in prayer, the Promise Keepers were able to gather 50,000 men in the University of Colorado's stadium in 1993 to proclaim their commitment to Jesus Christ. The growth continued in 1996 when the Promise Keepers held 22 renascence gatherings with more than a million men attending and organized a clergy conference in Atlanta attended by almost 40,000 men. In 1997, the conferences continued, culminating in Stand in the Gap: A Sacred Assembly of Men held on the Washington, D.C. mall in October. By 1998 the Promise Keepers message had become a mainstay in the evangelical community.

The following chapters form a *bricolage* of the Promise Keepers. A *bricolage* is formed when meaningful aspects concerning a subject are joined together to form one totalization. This is not the only totalization that could have been written. A *bricolage* is not like buying a tour package on Carnival Cruise Lines where one's observations and activities are mapped out before one sets sail. Instead, a *bricolage* is more like a road trip. One has an idea, a form of transportation, and an interest in going somewhere. The road trip, like the cruise, has a beginning and an end, but the means of observation and the activities are less determined and more aleatory. In other words, I can extend or curtail the road trip at any moment, pursuing observations and activities more or less to their fruition; the cruise line confines my observations and activities to the port calls and schedule. My time with the Promise Keepers has been more like a road trip than a cruise. I pursued thoughts and observations until they clarified themselves. I attended stadium events, training sessions, and small group meetings until I had an understanding of how they worked. I talked to men until I grasped the impact Promise Keepers was having on their lives. The product of this road trip is a *bricolage* of the Promise Keepers, various aspects of the movement pursued independently that form a particular totalization.

The chapters describe five aspects of the Promise Keepers movement. The first chapter looks at how stadium events and small group meetings are fundamental to the "making of" a Promise Keeper. The second details the Promise Keepers organization and its founder, Bill McCartney, by looking at evangelicalism and the PK Team. The third chapter employs the notion of social capital to analyze the practice of promise keeping. The fourth discusses the importance of a stable male (masculine) identity. The fifth chapter is based on a

39 hour bus trip with 50 men to the sacred assembly in Washington, D.C. The five chapters can be read individually; theoretically, the reader should be able to read them in any order. This does not mean that there is no logic in ordering the readings as they are presented, only that each chapter should be viewed from its own strengths and limitations.

I have used a variety of methodologies in researching the Promise Keepers. Information was gathered through both indepth and summary interviews, study of the literature of and about the movement, and nonparticipant observation. The nonparticipant observations include attendance at two accountability groups (total of eight visits), Key Man and Ambassador training, a PK clergy and church leader gathering, four stadium conferences, and the sacred assembly in Washington, D.C.

In identifying individual Promise Keepers I have only used first names. When I talk about a particular group (such as the "New Bethel" group in Gary, Indiana), I have substituted a fictitious name for the group and for the men involved. The men never made such a request, it was only done in order to provide a degree of anonymity.

# Chapter One

## Politics and Promises

"Bryan, do you know the Lord?"

I had anticipated and encountered this question on several occasions when meeting with Promise Keepers, and usually with the same sincerity as Bill's query. Bill, the son of a pastor and raised in Gary, Indiana, is a remarkable man I met at a Promise Keepers accountability group. He is a black man, church deacon, business manager, husband, and father. Bill is remarkable because of his calmness of character; he exhibits the serenity of sincere Christian faith.

Perhaps, from a sociopolitical perspective, Bill embodies all that is good about Christianity. He is a loyal husband, a concerned father, and active in his church and community. Bill is a leader. There is a calmness that surrounds him. It is the kind of serenity one finds when the murkiness of the world dissipates before one's eyes and one begins clearly to understand one's surroundings. Bill is at peace in his world; he lives in harmony. Bill's Christian faith provides the lens through which he views the world, perhaps similar to the way political scientists rely on party identification to understand how a party member views politics. Bill uses the Bible as his perceptual screen to filter information from his surroundings.

But Bill and other Promise Keepers differ from a typical Democrat or Republican in that they consider the Bible to be the final word on an issue, whereas one's party identification is only a reference point when one has no position on an issue. When evangelical Christians use the Bible, they seek an appropriate translation (interpretation) of God's word. For Bill, there is no doubt about the accuracy and truthfulness of the Bible; it is the word of God.

Bill's question was intended neither to intimidate nor to threaten, but was an inquiry based on a concern and a willingness to understand my relationship with

Christ. The question was a hailing, what Louis Althusser called an "interpellation."[1] According to Promise Keepers, we all have a relationship with Christ; some are saved and some are yet to be saved. Bill's question was personal; he wanted to know if I was saved.

In typical evangelical fashion, the "do you know the Lord?" question is usually asked during the first meeting with a Promise Keeper, or shortly thereafter.[2] It is the starting point. It raises the issue of brokenness. It is how a Promise Keeper begins to organize and understand his world. If the addressed individual responds with something similar to "Yes, I have a personal relationship with the Lord," the man becomes an acquaintance; a potential brother in Christ. If the answer is no or an attempt to avoid any direct response, the man is considered a not-yet-believer, someone the Promise Keeper can witness to and encourage since the not-yet-believer undoubtedly seeks to know the Lord.

The "do you know the Lord?" poses the first of a series of "political" inquiries to be conducted in this chapter. The Promise Keepers characterize themselves as a nonpolitical movement. This produces a question: what does "nonpolitical" mean? Does it include apolitical? Antipolitical? Does it really imply something similar to politics, a contesting of values?

Promise Keepers focus is outlined in their mission (also called "purpose") statement: "Promise Keepers is a Christ-centered ministry dedicated to uniting men through vital relationships to become godly influences in their world." They claim to be a biblical men's ministry without political objectives. In a publication describing Stand in the Gap: A Sacred Assembly of Men held on the Washington, D.C. mall in October 1997, Randy Phillips, the president of Promise Keepers, states that the gathering "is a presentation from the church to Almighty God, without any political agenda, and it is convened by Jesus Christ."[3]

But claiming to have no political agenda and not having political potential are two different things. To differentiate between the two does not imply that the Promise Keepers are being disingenuous, naïve, or surreptitious concerning their intentions (all of which could be true); it does at least mean they have a different understanding of what it means to be political.

When Bill McCartney asks men to make a personal commitment to Jesus Christ and to accept him as their Savior, it does not concern politics. When Dr. Tony Evans tells men not to *ask* for the leadership of their family back, but to *take it back*, it is not about politics.[4] When Charles Colson warns men that American culture is collapsing and that "it is of life-and-death importance to this nation," it is not about politics.[5] When Pastor Raleigh Washington tells men "to establish committed relationships across racial lines," it is not about politics.[6]

According to the Promise Keepers, all of these issues may have been politicized, but they are not political. This is how Promise Keepers defend their movement as being nonpolitical. Politics is about issues that are open to discussion; issues that are debatable. Politics is *not* about the immutable. More accurately, politics should not debate that which is timeless: God's word.

Bill McCartney, in a letter to men attending the stadium conferences and/or sacred assembly, characterized the 1997 conference season in the following manner:

> Dear Men,
>
> The Lord is doing a new thing in our midst in 1997. He is taking us deeper – as a ministry and as individuals. As we grant the Holy Spirit access to every area of our lives, I believe He will guide us into uncharted waters. God is calling for our total commitment.[7]

These sentences are full of what many commentators would call political discourse, and they are typical of Promise Keepers literature: ministry, individual, "access to every area of our lives," to "guide us into uncharted waters," and total commitment. They focus on the individual's relation to spirituality and to specific actions implied by such a relationship. As political statements, they may not fall within a traditional definition of politics that implies organized procedural activity, such as voter registration drives or the lobbying of Congress, but they are political in a wider sense of being relevant to issues that are processed in the political system that is structured by such procedural activities.

The second point of the Promise Keepers Statement of Faith reads as follows: "We believe that the Bible is God's written revelation to man and that it is verbally inspired, authoritative, and without error in the original manuscript."[8] As individuals who take the Bible as the word of God, the Promise Keepers are not inclined to question that which appears to them as common sense and God's truth. In a formal way, this ends politics understood as discussion. There is little to debate if one has the truth, only the tactics of living by, accepting, and implementing the truth. The Promise Keepers do not think every situation is political. It may be politicized, but it is not political. If one thinks that every position is political, one does not know the truth of the Lord.

In a democratically based social order, the values espoused are supposedly open to discussion. Since the polis no longer exists, modern democratic states have developed democratic practices to discuss the policies the state will enforce. Democratic politics is inherently a discussion about the processes and policies that underscore social values. It is rarely about truth, but it is always already about values. The U.S. government is based on the Constitution, which outlines processes, and a Bill of Rights, a document of declared values. Some maintain that the documents may have been divinely inspired, but for the sake of argument, let us assume the documents derive from human resourcefulness. Therefore, taken as human documents, they are subject to human error and opportunities for revision and modification.

As an example, a recent survey found that 27 percent of Americans believe the 1st Amendment goes too far in protecting the rights it guarantees. Amending the 1st Amendment is a real possibility because the Constitution contains procedures for doing so; amending the Bible would be quite difficult, there are no procedures for amending God's word. For instance, imagine someone suggesting a new account of the creation of Adam and Eve. Instead of God creating Eve from Adam's rib, one could suggest a revision that takes into account today's egalitarian and politically correct society: God made them both at the same time. Perhaps the story of Eve's deception by the snake coiled in the tree of the knowledge of good and evil could be amended to protect Eve and all women from being marked as a sex that easily succumbs to deception, not to mention appeasing the animal rights groups for the bad reputation snakes have suffered from this infamous deception. The story of Cain killing Abel could be revised; today's story would call for a therapist to discuss Cain's jealousy toward his brother.

All of this could happen; some of it is already in "updates" by some groups. But the ideological point is important. The Bible has a truth principle that is beyond interpretation for many individuals and groups, the Promise Keepers included.

If the Bible is the source of God's truth, then spreading the word of God becomes an evangelical organization's primary focus. For the Promise Keepers, this task begins when men admit their brokenness, accept Jesus Christ into their lives, and form vital relationships with a few other men.

In order to spread their message with clarity, the Promise Keepers produce stadium conferences, recommend the formation of men's small groups, and conduct training sessions for Key Men and Ambassadors.

I attended a Promise Keepers Level One training session for Ambassadors. The training is a two-and-a-half-hour session detailing the role of an Ambassador, how to relate to and recruit Key Men, and how to communicate the mission of Promise Keepers to local congregations, in particular, to parish and lay leaders. Ambassadors are voluntary representatives of Promise Keepers. An Ambassador must be recommended by his pastor and approved by the Promise Keepers national Ambassadors office.[9]

The role of an Ambassador is further discussed in the following chapter, but how Promise Keepers instructs the Ambassadors to rely on the Bible to clarify (and avoid) politicizing issues is instructive at this point. The following excerpts are taken from the Ambassador Training Level One manual used at the training session. It recommends that the Ambassador rely on the Purpose Statement, as well as the Statement of Faith and the Seven Promises, to answer questions others may have about Promise Keepers positions on contemporary social problems. The manual offers the following examples:

A. Avoid going outside the purpose statement as you are approached with questions.

1. Example 1: "What is Promise Keepers going to do about all the single mothers in our country?" You might answer, "If you look at our purpose statement you will see that we are called to uniting men in vital relationships. As we do that, we are seeing that men find out what it is to live as a godly man and in doing so will begin to meet the needs of single mothers."

2. Example 2: "Isn't Promise Keepers really anti-homosexual?" You might answer, "Our statement of faith clearly states that we believe the Bible is the Word of God, so in areas where the Bible clearly speaks to an issue, we must agree with it. Our purpose statement says clearly that we are committed to uniting men; therefore men who are struggling with homosexuality are welcome at our gatherings."[10]

The problem of "all the single mothers in our country" can be resolved by imparting to men an understanding of biblical responsibility and integrity, a different interpellation if you will. Instead of a man who will father a child and then absolve himself of any responsibility for the care of the family, Promise Keepers calls on men to accept the interpellation of a godly man – one who accepts the responsibilities of a father as defined in the Bible. As men learn to live as godly men, the needs of single mothers will be met. The question and problem are addressed not by discussing contemporary sexual standards, issues of birth control, or taxes to support single mothers and the children; instead, Promise Keepers returns to a biblical foundation ("a godly man") in order to resolve the issue.

In the second example, the same pattern is visible. Promise Keepers is not antihomosexual; they are pro-Bible. Since the Bible is clear (according to Promise Keepers) about the sin of homosexuality, it is not a political issue. Men who are "struggling with homosexuality" and "committed to uniting with men" are welcome at Promise Keepers gatherings in the same way as are other sinners.

In both examples, the Ambassador is instructed on possible ways to avoid discussing issues outside Promise Keepers biblical foundations. In both cases the Bible is used to depoliticize the social *bricolage*.[11] Instead of politicizing single mothers, absent fathers, and sexuality, the Promise Keepers simplify the issues down to a biblical understanding. In doing so, the controversial is replaced with the incontestable, the debatable with the immutable, and the political with the truth.

Promise Keepers is only an apolitical organization if one relies on a limited definition of what it means to be political. The effort to depoliticize issues such as "the needs of single mothers" and homosexuality is based on Promise Keepers interpretation of the Bible. On the one hand, the move is strategic;

Promise Keepers is able to avoid contentious political debates while remaining focused on its evangelical mission.

But, on the other hand, the evangelical mission focuses on an individual's walk with the Lord. As men return to the Lord's ways, perceived social concerns will be resolved through spiritual renewal. The depoliticization of social issues makes the Promise Keepers effectively antipolitical. They are effectively antipolitical if political means public (group) action. The leaders of Promise Keepers are often involved in political agendas, which are discussed in the following chapter, but that does not mean the men involved at the local level (in their churches and men's groups) share the leaders' political agendas. They are not mere puppets of the national leadership.

The rest of the chapter looks at the consciousness raising of a Promise Keeper and how politics is exhibited in the practice. It describes how stadium events and men's small groups function as the focal points of interpellation. It also points to a difference between politics as public activity and politics as prayer. For Promise Keepers at a local level, political matters are prayed about rather than acted on, or they are lightened with humor and otherwise avoided. If one negates God's influence through prayer (a big negation for believers), then politics as prayer becomes antipolitics.

## Consciousness Raising

> People who are without names, who do not know themselves, who have no culture, experience a kind of paralysis of consciousness. The first step is to connect and learn to trust one another.
>
> Sheila Rowbotham, *Woman's Consciousness, Man's World*

> Brothers are the sons of a common Father. They are heirs of a common spiritual inheritance, so brothers should be there for one another. Brothers should stand together and take care of one another.
>
> Promise Keepers, *Man of His Word Bible*

The men stand together, join hands, and prepare to sing a song of praise. Joseph is the designated praise leader. He supplies the short songs of praise, often writing them during the prayer request time. The men like to make fun of their singing ability, stating something similar to "the Lord does not mind our singing as long as we are singing to him." The following is Joseph's song of praise on this day:

> Lord, you are more precious than silver,
> Lord, you are more costly than gold,
> Lord, you are more beautiful than diamonds,
> And nothing I desire compares with you.
> (repeated)

Typical of born-again Christians, this is an emotive part of the morning. The men raise their hands in praise, adlibbing to the song with comments such as "Praise Jesus" or "Yes Lord." Their hands shake and they find it hard to stand still. It is quite moving, literally and emotionally. The men are feeling the Lord and the Holy Spirit. It is a sincere expression of their relationship with Christ. It would be easy to dismiss this as comical if it did not mean so much to the men. At first it was strange to witness. I had to get over my own prejudices. If one takes it from their perspective, it is how the Lord and the Holy Spirit play a vital role in their lives.

On this particular day, Harold begins with a personal variation of the Lord's Prayer. This is followed by Walter who gives an emotional testimony of how his niece only the day before had accepted the Lord. His voice cracks and he fights back tears. He also mentions a woman who was near death and, through prayer and the Lord's will, is now recovering at home. Walter also thanks the Lord for raising him from his slumber and for giving him a new day. (Later on in today's discussion Ed states that it is the Lord who wakes you in the morning, not the alarm clock, and continues that if you put the alarm clock in a mortuary, it does not have the power to wake the dead; only the Lord can do that.) Ed, Joseph, and Don then complete the prayer session by praying for the requests discussed earlier in the session.

The praise session described above is an effort to bring the men closer together as a group and closer to God's work. It is part of Promise Keepers main effort, what I will refer to as "biblical consciousness raising." It may seem strange to think that men need their group status discussed, or that men as a group need to rally and discuss what it means to be a man. But this is exactly what happens at Promise Keepers events. To accomplish this interpellation, Promise Keepers use all forms of modern technology, including video messages, prayer-a-grams over e-mail, Internet websites, infomercials on television, daily and weekly radio messages, and stadium conferences. But if organization is a form of technology, in that it prepares people to act a certain way, then the most compelling technology prescribed by the Promise Keepers are the stadium events and the men's small group Bible study.

The feminist movement is often criticized by the Promise Keepers, but their criticism does not mean that they have refused to learn from the often successful organizational techniques made popular by the feminist movement, in particular, consciousness raising sessions. Women meeting in small groups to discuss what it meant to be a woman were a hallmark of the feminist movement in the sixties and seventies. Catharine MacKinnon, a prominent feminist scholar, even claims that consciousness raising is the definitive element of the feminist method.[12] MacKinnon defines consciousness raising as the "collective critical reconstitution of the meaning of women's social experience, as women live through it."[13] Consciousness raising sessions allow women the opportunity of self-definition, a temporary 'free space.' The group atmosphere provides an opportunity for transforming and defining one's identity with the support of like-minded individuals. It is not an ideologically free space, but an opportunity to investigate, challenge, and transform one's identity and ideology in certain different directions.

Consciousness raising sessions were also an effort to promote intimacy between women in order to facilitate communication. Jane De Hart Mathews, a historian, describes the development of the group's emotional closeness in the following manner: "the immediate task of the consciousness raising session was to bring together in a caring, supportive, non competitive setting women accustomed to relating most intimately not with other women but with men – husbands, lovers, 'friends.'"[14] Consciousness raising sessions allow women the opportunity to form relationships, share experiences, and often to develop a sense of shared problems and concerns.

The Promise Keepers also understand the importance of having the support of like-minded individuals and the formation of sustaining intimate relationships. The second promise of a Promise Keeper is to be "committed to pursue vital relationships with a few other men, understanding that he needs his brothers to help him keep his promises."[15] A Promise Keeper needs his brothers because of man's broken relationship with God. Since the fall, man cannot be a promise keeper without the support of and accountability to his brothers. A man alone succumbs to the weight of the world; he cannot keep his promises because in his isolation from God and his brothers he will inevitably yield to temptation. Similar to the consciousness raising sessions used by the women's movement, only with a different ideological focus, the Promise Keepers find safety, encouragement, and growth in the context of relationship:

> Safety from temptation – In secret it has power over us, but when shared, we gain the victory.
>
> Encouragement – I'm not alone; I will take heart and go on.
>
> Growth – Regular interaction with the Bible and being held accountable by a friend will result in measurable steps toward spiritual maturity. Even the Lone Ranger had a friend.[16]

"Even the Lone Ranger had a friend."

In order to pursue vital relationships with a few other men, the Promise Keepers recommend the formation of a small men's Bible study group, a biblical consciousness raising session if you will. The small group allows the men to overcome their cultural and natural tendency to be 'loners.' The Promise Keepers cite the work of Carol Gilligan, a psychologist, to support their position: "Women view closeness in positive ways, men view it as a threat. On the other hand, women view social distance as abandonment, but men view it as safety."[17] According to the Promise Keepers, men have a problem with intimacy; men like to be alone and are uncomfortable with emotional closeness.

The cause of this lack of intimacy is both cultural and natural. Culture has taken the Lone Ranger image, personified as the male mystique, producing an unnatural outcome of too many men identifying with and trying to live by the Lone Ranger imago.[18] But, for the Promise Keepers, lacking desire for intimacy is just a natural stage in the growth of men. Too many men remain stuck in this stage, thereby missing the developing maturity found in intimate relationships with other men. For the Promise Keepers, men need the support of a small men's group in order to witness the potential impact of intimacy for growth and maturity.

MacKinnon defined consciousness raising as the "collective critical reconstitution of the meaning of women's social experience, as women live through it." If one deletes the "wo" from the "women" in the definition, one has a working definition of what the Promise Keepers are attempting to do: the collective critical reconstitution of the meaning of *men's* social experience, as *men* live through it.

But there is an important difference besides the subtraction of "wo." The difference is in the use of the word "critical." In MacKinnon's definition, critical seems to mean a careful and exact evaluation, to judge severely. The women's movement focused their critical reconstitution through the lens of societal inequality. The Promise Keepers render the same effect, but with a different "perceptual filter." Feminist critical reconstitution is through the structural lens of social equality; the Promise Keepers critical reconstitution is performed through the poststructural lens of culture. One could say the driving force supporting both movements is a will to power, the power to define one's immediate horizon. Said another way, the former focuses on an analysis of structural social inequality[19] while the latter on an analysis of poststructural cultural degradation of biblical values. Therefore a summary definition of (men's) biblical consciousness raising would be: The collective *biblical* reconstitution of the meaning of men's social experience, as men live through it.

The different focal points do not invalidate the numerous similarities between the women's movement and the Promise Keepers. For example, MacKinnon suggests that "consciousness raising groups were many women's first explicit contact with acknowledged feminism."[20] The Promise Keepers believe that many men no longer know what it means to be a godly man, to experience the love of Christ, or the truth of God's word.

MacKinnon states that the consciousness raising groups were grassroots efforts that "aimed for diversity in age, marital status, occupation, education, physical ability, sexuality, race and ethnicity, class, or political views."[21] The Promise Keepers maintain and promote similar egalitarian positions; the sixth promise is to reach beyond any racial and denominational barriers to demonstrate the power of biblical unity. The Promise Keepers also believe they "have a God-given mission to unite Christian men who are currently separated by race, sectarianism, age, culture, and economics."[22]

According to MacKinnon, small women's groups find enough shared experiences to provide a basis for identification and that "women's lives are discussed in all their momentous triviality, that is, as they are lived through."[23] This experience allows the women to know that they are not alone and to find support for common concerns within the group. The Promise Keepers believe that men's groups need to focus on building relationships (promise two) because "when men feel comfortable in an atmosphere of safety, they will open up and be authentic."[24] In 'opening up' the men begin to share their testimony, ranging from the triviality of childhood experiences to the most painful experiences of adulthood.

The final similarity between feminist and Promise Keepers practices is the absence of the other sex. MacKinnon, while discussing feminist consciousness raising sessions, states that "the fact that men were not physically present was usually considered necessary to the process . . .," since "it made speech possible."[25] The Promise Keepers maintain the same exclusionary element, stating that "effective men's ministries are restricted to men only."[26] This is because "men need an environment where they can share their weaknesses, struggles, triumphs and challenges just with men."[27] This view was echoed in a conversation with Harold, a 71-year-old Promise Keeper, who said "men will tell things to another man that they would never tell to a woman; especially their wife."

There is always an Other. Simone de Beauvoir connected otherness to consciousness itself. In *The Second Sex* she wrote that "no group ever sets itself up as One without at once setting up the Other over against itself."[28] She also said "A man would never get the notion of writing a book on the peculiar situation of the human male."[29] She is correct in the first case, but the recent men's movement disputes her second point.

But what is consciousness without performativity. Judith Butler suggests that too often individuals think of sex and sexuality as either constructed or determined. She argues such either/or ideals elide the performativity of sex and sexuality. Butler calls one's attention to the complexity of "the conditions under which sex and sexuality are assumed."[30] The complexity, the performative dimension of sex and sexuality, is witnessed in the "forced reiteration of norms."[31] This process of iterability enables men to perform, to be men. The ritual interaction (Promise Keepers gathering together on a regular basis to discuss issues pertaining to men) produces within the group the One as opposed to the Other; it is how/why Harold can tell men things he could never tell a woman, especially his wife.

The discussion of the similarities and differences between the feminists' method of consciousness raising and the Promise Keepers promotion of men's small groups has been an effort to show how Promise Keepers convey their message of biblical truth. But before I discuss the men's small groups in more detail, it is necessary to discuss how the Promise Keepers get the men to want to participate in a small group in the first place. How are the men hailed/called/interpellated to identify themselves as promise breakers and not promise keepers? In other words, what is the catalyst that convokes the desire to form vital relationships with a few other men?

## Stadium Conferences

The following is excerpted from *The Night that Changed Our Lives*, a story highlighted in the brochure for the 1997 Promise Keepers Conference season:

> It was well after midnight when Jackie Kline heard the car pull up. Her husband Jack was returning from a Promise Keepers conference in St. Petersburg. She rolled over, pretending to sleep.
>
> So many years had passed since she had even felt married to Jack. They shared nothing, discussed nothing. He did his thing; she did hers. Yet, as she heard Jack's footsteps in the hallway, an odd expectancy welled up in her. She prayed for so long that God would work a miracle in their marriage, but this? – how could a men's conference possibly make a difference?
>
> Jack tiptoed into the bedroom and lay stiffly beside Jackie. Awkward moments passed. Then, almost too softly to feel, he reached out and touched the ends of her hair caressing it hesitantly – like a child. Then, just as hesitantly, he pulled back. Jackie's heart was pounding. Lord, what's going on? She knew Jack was a man of few words. Can it be? Is he reaching out? She turned to find his face wet with tears. With quavering voice, he whispered, "Honey. . . I am sorry. I don't know how to ask. Can. . . can you ever forgive me?" As if in direct response to her prayers, the hardness that had scarred her heart now suddenly, miraculously, dissolved. She pulled Jack close as they both burst into tears. They held one another, crying, laughing and talking until morning.[32]

The stadium conferences are the catalyst used by the Promise Keepers to raise men's biblical consciousness. The conferences are designed as interpellation events. They call on each man to examine and fulfill his life from a biblical perspective. In a straightforward manner, the conference is designed to ask men if they have kept their promises: "Hey, you there! Have you kept your promises?"

Jack, in the preceding story, is an example of a man who attended a conference and had a proselytizing (existential) experience. He had grown apart from his wife, which undermined his marriage vow, and the conference called him to examine his commitments.

The conferences are structured in order to make men think about their promises. Questions are posed from the stage by various speakers, with the intent of distilling biblical values from cultural ones, often with the production of shame and guilt for having failed. The interpellations of shame and guilt are always followed by the reconciling and hopeful message of Jesus Christ.

Typically, queries focus on a biblical understanding of what it means to be a godly man. The men are asked: Do you support your wife? Are you a good husband? Do you have a relationship with Christ? Are you struggling with homosexuality, pornography, or lust? Do you judge others without showing them the love of Christ? Are you a racist? A denominationalist? Do you spend time with your children? How have you failed your wife? Children? Brothers? Community?

"To know that I'm not alone – that, in itself, was an encouragement."
Sam Caldwell, Everett, WA.[33]

The "do you know the Lord?" question is the Promise Keepers standard interpellation-hail. It 'recruits' men to take a position on their relationship with Jesus Christ. Paraphrasing Althusser's example of religious ideology, Promise Keeper ideology says something like this:

> It says: I address myself to you, a man called [put your name here], in order to tell you that God exists, you are answerable to Him, and that he gave his only Son so that you may be saved. It adds: God addresses himself to you through the Bible, God's word, and the Holy Spirit. It says: this is who you are: you are [put your name here]! This is your origin, you were created by God for all eternity, although you were born in [insert year] of Our Lord! This is your place in the world! This is what you must do! By these means, if you observe the 'law of love' you will be saved, you, [put your name here], and will become part of the Glorious Body of Christ! Etc. . . .

Not everyone accepts the hail immediately. There are the resistors, or what the Promise Keepers call the not-yet-believers. There are at least four common responses, all of which call a man into a relationship with Jesus Christ. The following are ordered from a strong relationship with Christ to one that denies the need for the saving grace of Jesus:

1. Yes, I know the Lord.
2. I'm unsure of my commitment to the Lord.
3. No, who is he?
4. No, I don't need his sacrifice.

Once the man responds to the hail, the 'Hey, you,' the interpellation begins. If the response is similar to number one, the men can grow and mature in their relationship with the Lord. If response number two, the men can begin to discuss Jesus and witness to the man's doubts. If number three, the Christians can tell the not-yet-believer about the love and salvation found in the teachings of Jesus Christ. If the response is similar to number four, the Christians focus on criticizing the attempt to go it alone (Lone Ranger) or to live by other salvations (money, success, self-interest).

Excerpt from introduction to PK *Man of His Word*, New Testament, 1996, Ephesians 2:12:

> We have inherited a diseased spiritual DNA. It's no wonder we find failure and sin in our lives today. It is by our choices that we continue to exist outside a relationship with God.
>
> This leaves us without the bonds of communion with our Father that all of us are meant to have. The ties we have cut. This alienation is described in the New Testament as being "separate from Christ . . . without hope and without God in the world."[34]

For many men, biblical consciousness raising begins at the stadium conferences. Of course, they have already been motivated to attend the conference. It could be the suggestion of one's wife (in the case of Jack above), curiosity, the urging of friends, the inability to say no to friends, or the search for a purpose. Whatever the reason, an explicit call is announced at the conference.

On this night, 60,000 men are asked if they know the Lord, do they know the love of the Lord, do they have a relationship with Jesus, do they understand that Christ died for their sins, are they ignoring the truth of God and leading a sinful life, do they know Satan better than Jesus, have they turned their backs on their Father?

During the altar call (the ultimate 'Hey you' procedure), a regular Friday night occurrence at stadium conferences that is led from the stage, the men are asked to come down from their seats, forward to the stage, and to proclaim their acceptance or rededication to Jesus Christ.

At first, a few men step forward, both individually and in small groups. Then the speaker on the stage urges each man to turn to the man next to him and tell him "you'll go forward with him if he needs a brother."

The men are told that this is their chance to accept the redeeming love and to acknowledge the sacrifice of Jesus Christ. "Is there a reason good enough to keep you from accepting Jesus Christ as your Savior?"

As the men continue to go forward, often in pairs, the men who have filled the stadium begin to sing Amazing Grace as the words appear on the Jumbotron:

> Amazing Grace, how sweet the sound
> That saved a wretch like me
> I once was lost but now am found
> Was blind, but now I see
> 'Twas grace that taught my heart to fear
> And grace my fears relieved
> How precious did that grace appear
> The hour I first believed

Once the majority of those going forward are in front of the stage, on this night approximately 3,000 men, the stadium is led in prayer. After this, the men who have gone forward form into groups of five or six, irrespective of race and age, and are counseled and led in prayer by an "evangelism volunteer." The men are then led through the following:

**Understanding Your Commitment**

**The Good News: God Loves His Sons**
*"For God so loved the world [put your name here]
that he gave his one and only Son."*
John 3:16

**Reconciliation With God Is Through Christ**
*"God was reconciling the world to himself in Christ"*
2 Corinthians 5:19

**Mankind Lost A Relationship Through Sin**
*"For as in Adam all die"*
1 Corinthians 15:22

**We Need A Restored Relationship To God**
*"How shall we escape if we ignore such a great salvation?"*
Hebrews 2:3

**Jesus Christ Forgives Our Sin. He Restores Us To Our Father God**
*"Yet to all who received him, he gave the right to become children of God."*
John 1:12

**Pray This Prayer To Accept or Reaffirm Your Acceptance Of Christ:**
*Father, I've come home. Please make me your son. I turn from my sin. I accept your forgiveness made possible through Jesus Christ by his death and resurrection. I place my faith and trust in Jesus Christ alone. I receive him as my Savior and Lord. I want to follow and serve you. Let today be the beginning of my new journey as your son and a member of your family. You have always kept your promises. Help me to keep my promises, too. In Jesus' name. Amen.*

**Welcome To The Family Of God!**

- Please talk with an evangelism volunteer near you.
- Fill out the decision card on the opposite page.
- Pray together.
- When you return home, find another man who will study the following pages together with you.[35]

The interpellation sequence: Hey, you; you are a son of God; and even though you are a sinner, you can be reconciled to God through Christ; yes, I am a sinner; I need a restored relationship to God; Christ forgives my sins; I accept Christ; He can help me keep my promises; When I return home, I will study the Bible with another man.

The decision card can be filled out by the men who go forward and by the men who remain in their seats. Obviously, there is not enough room for everyone to go forward. The card is included in the copy of the Promise Keepers *Man of His Word*, New Testament, that each man receives as he enters the stadium.

The decision card asks the men to check the statement that best describes their commitment:

❑ ACCEPTANCE
I want to become a son of God. I trust Jesus Christ to be my Savior and Lord.

❑ REDEDICATION
I believe that I am a son of God, but I have been walking my own way. I want to renew my commitment to Jesus Christ.

❑ OTHER
I want someone to pray with me.
I want to trust God to intervene in my situation. Here is my need:[36]

The card also asks the men for their address, their phone number, if they attend church, and their church affiliation.

Toward the end of the interview I asked Jim why he attends Promise Keepers conferences. I had prefaced this question by saying that he seemed to be happily married, a successful businessman, and that he appeared already to have a strong relationship with Jesus. Why did he still attend Promise Keepers conferences?

Jim said that for some people Promise Keepers conferences are an introduction to the renewing spirit of Christ. He began telling me about the last conference he had attended and the time he had spent with Jonathon, a young man who was terribly unsettled by the conference. Jim said he and Jonathon had a long discussion about what was troubling him. Jonathon told Jim that he had just realized how badly he had been neglecting his marriage commitment. He had failed his wife; not out of hatred or a lack of will, but because he had turned his back on Jesus Christ. Jim said he and Jonathon prayed for God to give Jonathon the strength to live up to his biblical commitments.

Jim went on to say that the conferences are a refreshing experience for him. He offered a sports analogy to explain. He compared being a Christian to being a golfer and baseball player. He said that a golfer has to keep working on the basics, to keep practicing the fundamentals – because it is the little things that make it all come together. He said baseball players still go to spring training, that they must continue to work on the finer points of hitting and fielding. For Jim, the conferences provide a refresher course on the basics; they augment and nourish his faith. Jim said that it was an invigorating experience to witness so many Christian men coming together to worship the Lord. For him, Promise Keepers is like a continuing education class; it refines and reminds while also providing the encouragement to continue on in one's faith.

The following is 1997 conference program, *The Making of a Godly Man.*

| | | |
|---|---|---|
| **Friday:** | | |
| **Clergy Conference for Men** | | |
| 8:30 am – 1:00 pm | | Becoming an Agent of Renewal |
| **The Heart of a Godly Man** | | |
| 6:30 pm – 10:00 pm | Session 1 | The Heart of a Godly Man: Captured by Christ |
| | Session 2 | Purity of Heart: Living Clean before God |
| **Saturday:** | | |
| **The Disciplines of a Godly Man** | | |
| 8:30 am – 12:00 pm | Session 3 | The Disciplines of a Godly Man: Motivate by Grace |
| | Practicum | Personal Financial Integrity: How to Get out of Debt |
| | Session 4 | Out of Isolation: Why a Men's Small Group? |
| **The Influences of a Godly Man** | | |
| 1:30 pm – 7:00 pm | Session 5 | The Influence of a Godly Man: A Servant Who Leads |
| | Practicum | A Man in the Workplace: Balancing Character and Competency |
| | Practicum | Going Public: How to Share Your Faith |
| | Session 6 | Embracing Reconciliation: Living Out the Great Commandment |
| | Final Wrap-up and Commission | Godly Men: Hope for Our Times[37] |

The interpellation process is incorporated into the structure and conduct of each session. At first, either prior to the start of the conference or during the break times, the men are milling around. Some are talking about Christianity, but more often than not it is simple "guy talk" – the weather, the local sports team, work, women.

1. Then the music begins. No one is singing yet, but the men realize that it is a cue that something is about to take place. They begin to take their seats, returning from the restrooms, concession vendors, or smoking areas.

2. Singing is led by an artist or the chorus on the stage. Sometimes, there are solos, with a Christian singer performing and the chorus supporting.

3. After one or two songs, the men in the stadium are asked to participate. The words are displayed on the Jumbotron or it is a song with which most Christian men are familiar.

4. Next, a video is viewed to illustrate the next theme. It calls the men to identify with failed commitments. At the 1996 stadium conferences, each video reflected a different theme. If the next session was on a man's commitment to his family, particularly his children, the video would depict children asking why their father couldn't make it to their ballgame, why dad fights with mom, or why dad is always too busy to spend time with them.

   The 1997 video series brings the themes together into a story line based on four men involved in a small men's group. The video focuses on the dynamics and themes relevant to group accountability and growth. The men vary in age and are of different races and economic groups. One man struggles with sexual sin, fearing the group will think less of him for admitting to a struggle with pornography. The other men have problems with alcohol, marriage, raising children, anger, finances, and adultery. The video is a spring board to the next session and speaker, a 'Hey, you' video.

5. The speaker is introduced by the master of ceremonies. The Promise Keepers have a mix of distinguished speakers for all of their conferences. Almost all of them are well known in the evangelical community. Often, the speakers have recently published a book that is on sale in the bookstalls set up around the stadium.

   The speakers use humor to get the men comfortable, not unlike other public speakers. The humor puts the audience at ease and prepares them for the main point of the session. As an example, Max Lucado, speaking on the importance of financial integrity for Christian men, told the following paraphrased joke at the 1997 St. Louis Conference:

   > A rich Christian man wanted to take some of his wealth to Heaven. He prayed to God, asking if God would allow it. God told him he would not need his wealth in Heaven since all of his needs would already be met. The rich man remained unconvinced and continued to beseech God. God finally relented and fulfilled the man's request; God told the man that he could bring one suitcase

> filled with the riches of his choice. The man prepared the suitcase and waited for the big day.
>
> When the day arrived, St Peter greeted the rich man at the pearly gates and said to him "Welcome to Heaven, but why the suitcase? You will have need of nothing here in Heaven."
>
> The rich man responded that God had told him it would be all right for him to bring one suitcase of his wealth to Heaven. Peter was somewhat skeptical, so he placed the suitcase on a table and opened it. Then he looked at the gold the man had placed in his suitcase; then he looked at the man; the suitcase; the man; the suitcase; the man. Finally, St Peter said with an air of disbelief, "Pavement? You brought pavement to Heaven?"

After the audience is relaxed and prepared for the message, the body of the presentation hooks the listeners. It grabs them. Centering on verses from the Bible, the presentation calls the audience to understand how they have failed their promises and how God can forgive their past sins and help them overcome their future failings.

The presenter always closes with a message of hope. Men, such as Jack, are not left with a feeling of lonely helplessness, but rather of redeeming hopefulness. Sure, they have failed in the past, but God understands. Confronting the sin is the first step toward reconciliation; allowing Christ into your life seals the deal.

6. The speaker then asks the men to come together and form groups of three and four with the men around them. They are asked to talk to the group about the session and to share any lessons they have learned. This is often an emotional time, since the men begin to discuss heartfelt concerns regarding marriage, children, race, and/or personal salvation.

   The men are then led in prayer by the presenter. This concludes the session and begins a break period.

## Men's Small Group Bible Studies

The Promise Keepers offer many "entry points" for men to get involved in a men's ministry, including men's stadium conferences, special events, equipping seminars, congregational gatherings, and small groups.[38] As suggested above, the stadium conferences are designed to hail the man into biblical consciousness, while, as will be discussed below, the men's small group continues to solidify the commitment and interpellation.

The small men's Bible study is designed to ride the wave of momentum generated by the stadium events.[39] Instead of the men only being motivated by the stadium gatherings and then having their biblical consciousness dissipate over the following weeks and months, Promise Keepers asks the men to form vital relationships with a few other men – they are asked to form a men's small group Bible study.

The workbooks *Applying the Seven Promises* and *The Promise Keeper At Work*, part of the Promise Builders series, describe various patterns of men's small group Bible studies, each based on the 'sea-worthiness' of a vessel. It is Promise Keepers hope that the men's group will focus "on interactive discussion and the application of the timeless insights of God's Word."[40] With such focus, the 'sea-worthiness' of the group plays a fundamental role in maintaining the biblical consciousness instilled at the stadium conference. According to Promise Keepers, "Men who gather in a small group to fellowship, study the Bible, and pray together predictably follow one of several patterns."[41] The patterns include:

1. "Adrift" – The Life Raft Group. Made up of men who have survived a major battle in their lives. Usually leaderless; each man with his own story. Usually lacking in biblical resources.

2. "Feeling Good" – The Yacht Group. A group based on fellowship with little biblical emphasis.

3. "Battle Weary" – The Destroyer Group. Ready to "battle against the forces of evil in a society." Disciplined Bible study; "Truth from Scripture is fired from the leader like missiles from the deck launchers."

4. "Deep and Long: Where Are We?" – The Submarine Group. Strategic Bible study "below the surface of life." Little fellowship; disciplined study.

5. "Refreshed, Refueled, Refocused" – The Carrier Group. Group has a mission. The weekly sessions allow the men time to "refresh, refuel, and refocus." The men leave the session "ready to fulfill the biblical plan they studied, alert to serve their Captain well."[42]

Promise Keepers believes the Carrier Group best serves the goal of becoming a man who can fulfill his biblical commitments. The strategic and combative analogy is based on how the men view their relationship to cultural influences in their own homes and at their places of work. 'Refreshed, Refueled, Refocused': refreshed to maintain a biblical perspective, refueled with the synergy of brotherly fellowship and biblical consciousness, and refocused (hailed) as a Christian man.

The introduction to the small group workbook *Applying the Seven Promises* answers the question, "What does it take for change to occur?" by stating; ". . .

time. Not just the ticking of the clock, but time that is given purposefully in this next year to study God's word with brothers in Christ and become accountable to each other."[43] The workbook, based on a year-long study, is broken into weekly lessons. Each lesson focuses on one of the Seven Promises and includes a warmup section, Scripture to be read, and questions for interaction. The lesson closes with a wrapup question, the promise restated, and a section titled "My response as a Promise Keeper," which includes two to three questions.

The introduction to the workbook concludes by describing what Promise Keepers hopes to accomplish in the small gathering of men:

> [Promise Keepers] is seeking to take the next step from the stadium to the small group. We believe that when men gather in the name of Jesus Christ, Almighty God is pleased. And when they gather weekly to fellowship, pray, and apply God's word, measurable change takes place. So call your friends, pick a place to meet, and go for it!
>
> "Be on your guard; stand firm in the faith; be men of courage; be strong. Do everything in love" (1 Cor. 16:13).[44]

The men gathered at the 1997 St. Louis stadium conference were told that the only thing that they could not take home from the conference were the men sitting around them. When they returned home, they also returned to the same friends, wife, habits, and culture. Dr. Joseph Stowell, president of Moody Bible Institute, called on the men to find another man committed to their spiritual success. Stowell advised the men that "everybody needs a God buddy."

T-shirt worn by a man attending the 1997 St. Louis stadium conference:
Friends Don't Let Friends
Go To HELL

The following discussion is a continuation of the praise and prayer session introduced at the beginning of this section. It is important to note that the men think of themselves as a "Promise Keepers men's group" and not just as a Christian men's group. They call themselves and each other Promise Keepers. They use the workbook *Applying the Seven Promises*. They go to the stadium conferences. Two of them are Key Men. They talk about Bill McCartney.

The "New Bethel" Church is located in Gary, Indiana. It is the host location for a 5:30 a.m. Promise Keepers men's group. Four of the six men regularly attending the men's group are also members of New Bethel Church. These four, Walter, Bill, Ed and Harold, are black men ranging in age from 44 (Walter) to 71 (Harold). The other two men, Don and Joseph, are white. The men often describe themselves as born-again Christians.

I attended the New Bethel group for seven consecutive Wednesday mornings during the spring of 1997. I met two of the men, Walter and Don, at the Promise

Keepers training for Key Men. At that time they discussed the success of their men's group in reaching beyond racial barriers and in facilitating new relationships. Don and Walter invited me to attend one of their group meetings and I accepted.

There is no evidence of racial tension within the group. Harold told me in one of our postgroup discussions that "all brothers look alike to him." Harold is implying that one's color does not matter; being a brother in Christ is what counts.

Don told me in a phone conversation that he had doubted whether he could ever grow close to black men. He said his father had been a "redneck" and that it took him years to grow out of the childish racist attitudes that were instilled in him by his father. He credited Promise Keepers for giving him the "push" he needed to complete his growth.

In a discussion on race, the men said that it is not enough just to have mixed churches if the men in the churches still do not talk to each other – the brotherhood is fundamental.

At my first session, Walter stated "We [as a group] are standing at second looking at the third base coach."

Joseph joked, "I don't know if I want to go any farther with you."

Walter and Joseph are referring to the "relational diamond" that is discussed in the workbook and used by Promise Keepers to show men how small groups usually develop. Trading on men's understanding of sports and on the underlying metaphor of sexual advancement, Promise Keepers organized a discussion of the growth of small groups to reflect a player's movement around a baseball diamond.

The relational diamond is a an example of Michel Foucault's discursive practice. As a practice, it systematically forms and orders the object, in this case, the workings of a Christian men's group.[45]

"Heading for First" involves defining the purpose and parameters of the group, to include the basics of who is in the group and when and where the group will meet. The men are encouraged to focus on listening skills and to work toward accepting one another. It is also recommended that the men commit to a "covenant of confidentiality."[46] When these guidelines and skills have been learned and acquired, the men have reached first base and are "Acquaintances."

"First Question: Who is speaking?" Michel Foucault's chapter "The Formation of Enunciative Modalities" focuses on the law operating behind statements, the practices that allow one to speak. The first practice is to sanction speech: Who is qualified to speak? In the Promise Keepers group the sanctioned are men who know the Lord.

"Sliding Into Second" involves a focus on "subjects men feel they need to discuss."[47] Examples include such questions as "What is true manliness? Is purity possible for the modern man? How can we nurture family life? What is biblical business conduct?"[48] The men are also encouraged to work on discussion and conflict resolution skills, including the "humility to confess to one another."[49] When they feel they have attained these skills, the men are "Friends."

The believer as friend. Foucault said of the doctor and the medical discourse that "We must also describe the institutional sites from which the doctor makes his discourse, and from which this discourse derives its legitimate source and point of application."[50] For the Promise Keepers, the institutional site is the church, the legitimate source is the Bible, and the point of application is the development of friendships in the group.

"Rounding Third" involves the men's growth from 'Friends' to 'Brothers.' This is accomplished by focusing on team building, worship, covenants, and accountability.[51] Some of the suggested covenants include 'The Covenant of Affirmation' ("I will love you and affirm you no matter what you have said or done."), 'The Covenant of Honesty' ("I will be honest in feedback to you in what I sense and feel coming from you."), and 'The Covenant of Accountability' ("You have the right to expect growth from me so that you may benefit from my gifts as I do yours. You have a right to ask me questions in that regard.").[52] The Promise Keepers counsel men that not everyone is ready for this level of commitment. The men should find a level of intensity with which the group is comfortable. Promise Keepers believe that men need accountability to other men, but that the covenant is always voluntary; men will benefit in proportion to their level of honesty.[53]

Brothers and the positioned subject. Foucault said "The positions of the subject are also defined by the situation that it is possible for him to occupy in relation to the various domains or groups of objects."[54] The use of covenants positions the subject in relation to the group, binding him to the object (in this case, his word). As Brothers, the men become Foucault's questioning, listening, and seeing subjects, both bound and binding. He is bound by his word and binds the other men in the group to the same enunciations.

"Coming Home," the final leg of the relational diamond, concentrates on building teamwork. With biblical guidance from the book of Acts, the men are encouraged to work on the Great Commandment (to love one another) and the Great Commission (to spread God's word). According to the Promise Keepers, "To become like Christ is to allow Him to change" the men "progressively from the inside out, to adopt His values" as the group's values.[55] 'Coming Home' is to become Christlike, a laborer in the Kingdom of God.[56]

Synthesis vs. dispersion. Foucault concluded "The Formation of Enunciative Modalities" by abandoning any attempt "to see discourse as a phenomenon of expression," of interiority, if you will. He describes the dispersed subject as a totality, a "space of exteriority in which a network of distinct sites is deployed."[57] The Promise Keepers synthesize that which Foucault warned against, but with their own ideological constructions. Foucault said "that it is neither by recourse to a transcendental subject nor by recourse to a psychological subjectivity that the regulation" of enunciations should be defined.[58] But the Promise Keepers, nonplussed by Foucault modalities, find a home in the recourse to both a transcendental subject (Christ) and to a psychological subjectivity (a laborer in the Kingdom of God).

In the middle of prayer requests, Ed abruptly stated that he was involved in a situation at work and that he did not know how to handle it. Ed is a board member for a local civic organization. He went on to explain that he was recently accused of giving away some confidential information on one of the members of the organization. The man began spreading rumors about Ed. With a heartfelt request for support, Ed asked the other five men for their prayers and support.

It is impossible to be sure of someone's honesty by perception and intuition, but, if anyone is, Ed is an exemplar of sincerity. He is a god-fearing Christian. When Bill asked me the "Do you know the Lord?" question, Ed followed with a sincere warning about how "unsaved souls burn in hell for eternity; and that's a long time."

The group responded to Ed with reassurance, comfort, and support. They were immediately concerned about Ed's well being, with the men on both sides of Ed reaching out to him and grasping his hands. The discussion was stopped and a prayer was said for Ed's situation.

Every session at New Bethel included prayer requests and prayer, followed by a song of praise. Prayer is the fundamental element that defines the group. Prayer summarizes their politics, give it to the Lord.

In the hour we would spend together, prayer requests, prayer, praise, and fellowship would take up 30 to 40 minutes of the group's time. The group always had to end promptly at 6:30 since four of the members had to leave for work.

The prayer requests facilitate the development of personal relationships between the men, since they open the discussion to the men's concerns. Prayer requests allow them to discuss their lives in a nonconfrontational manner as a way of coping with stress. The men can discuss anything of consequence to their life, from the intimidating to the innocuous. Common themes are sick friends or relatives, their own health, work experiences, or upcoming events in their lives.

Joseph asked everyone to pray for his relationship with his 14-year-old son. His exwife has custody and he rarely gets to see him. He prays for the opportunity to spend more time with his son; he wants "quality time because that equals quality relationships." He is concerned about his plan to take his son to the upcoming Promise Keepers stadium event in Chicago. Joseph may get to see him on the weekend of the event, his first opportunity since Christmas, and he does not want to distance him any more if he is not ready for the Lord. The others reassure Joseph that taking his son to a Promise Keepers conference may be exactly what the Lord intends to happen.

The men see (feel) the Lord and Holy Spirit at work in their daily lives. For 'not-yet-believers,' it may be difficult to understand the importance this experience has on their outlook. It calms them during difficult times and inspires them in mundane life. They posit (look for) intention, the Lord's will, in everything that happens to them.

Walter asked everyone to pray for Craig, a Christian man whom he met while waiting to have some work done on his car. Walter was reading the book *The Seven Promises of a Promise Keeper* and Craig began asking him questions about Promise Keepers. Craig was interested in the book because he had heard of Promise Keepers before and had previously attended a men's group. Both members of his group had moved because of their work, but he was interested in forming another small group. Craig told Walter that he missed the camaraderie of meeting with men. Walter invited him to attend the New Bethel group whenever he wanted to.

Joseph then asked for prayer for Ron, a friend of his with whom he tried to share the Gospel, but who was not ready to listen. He also requested prayer for his friend Thomas, a Jehovah's Witness, to whom Joseph began talking by telling him that he was praying for him. Joseph says that prayer always gets him pumped up. He also wanted to pray for the pastors and the leaders of the country. He said people sometimes forget the burdens and strains that the leaders must endure. Don chimed in that sometimes he deliberately tried to forget about the country's political leaders. A general chuckle followed.

Humor. The New Bethel group never discussed politics at length. Whenever politics intruded into the conversation, it was usually quickly dismissed with laughter. More than apolitical, the group was consistently antipolitical; anti-toward discussing politics either specifically or in general.

Joseph also requested prayer for Mark Weaver, a Congregationalist pastor who is planning on turning Orthodox within the year. This led to an exchange between Don and Joseph concerning Orthodox Russian churches not allowing Protestant churches into Russia. Joseph related a discussion he had with Mark concerning this issue, stating that the Orthodox churches were wary of the cultural influences that come with the western Protestant churches. Don then quipped in agreement that "Satan can sneak in anywhere."

Don then asked for prayer about the recent growth of his church's congregation. It seems that the building is too full for one Sunday service. The congregation either has to build or locate a larger building or begin to have two services on Sunday. Harold pointed out that such growth is also a blessing, since the congregation is reaching so many people.

Today's prayer request discussion focused on pornography and local adult bookstores. Don requested that everyone pray for the end of the growth of pornography and prostitution in his neighborhood, which is near a busy local intersection. After a brief discussion, everyone acknowledged the recent proliferation of sinful activities in that neighborhood. Bill related a story about a recent drive he took through that area on his way home from work; he was flashed by a woman who was walking down the street looking for business. Bill joked that he "just stepped on a pedal and hoped that it was the gas and not the brake!"

Bill said that perhaps this was one of the reasons why they were meeting as a group: perhaps they needed to go to these places and pray for them.

Politics intrudes. Bill, the undeclared leader of the group, suggests a political activity, a demonstration against pornography through public prayer.

There was a brief pause in the discussion. They seemed to hesitate when Bill suggested that they actually go to the stores and publicly pray against pornography.

Joseph broke the silence by relating a story about how some Christians had gone to strip clubs and prayed for the people there and in a short time the clubs closed. One had even recently been turned into a church.

Bill asked the group to begin praying for the eradication of pornography from their neighborhoods on a daily basis and then the group could see where the Lord would lead them. They also continued to pray for this on a weekly basis.

More prayer, but they did not go to the pornography store. Instead, they chose to place it (politics) into God's hands. Politics was confined to their prayers.

After the fellowship, prayer requests, prayer, and praise, the men begin the weekly lesson. While I visited them, they rarely completed a lesson during the allotted time. It usually took two to three meetings for them to cover the lesson.

The lesson today was the conclusion of last week's discussion of Luke 19:1-10 and the story of Zaccheus. They started in the section marked "My Response as a Promise Keeper." The question was the last in the lesson they had been working on for two weeks: "What evidence can be seen in my home that 'salvation has come to this house' (e.g. Unselfishness, honesty, goodwill, kindness)?"[59] Don began by stating they have an "open door policy" at his house. This means that anyone can stop by at any time. He quipped that they may not find him there, but anyone is welcome to stop by whenever necessary.

Joseph stated that, although his children do not always show it, he and his wife attempt to exhibit salvation and the Lord's work. He acknowledged that this is not always possible, but that they are committed to it as a standard.

Harold added that the most difficult sin to keep out of the home is sexual sin. He expressed disgust for sexual sin. He was passionate in his statement – a heartfelt conviction regarding the evils of sexual sin. He said that it was a sin against the body because it was selfish, a selfish act of indulgence. Sexual sin is "the worse kind of sin because it is self-focused. It does not think of others, only one's own pleasures." He added that sexual sin sets a bad example, especially for children. The other men seemed to agree with Harold, nodding agreement and support. Don added that the Bible says that pornography is a sin against the body. No one responded with the same energy as Harold.

Ed, still referring to the question, commented about the importance of witnessing to others. Whether it is at home or in the workplace, it is important and necessary for Christians to show others their love for the Lord.

The section ends by raising the question "If my house is not in order, then like Zaccheus, I will invite Jesus to help loosen my grip on my money and my goods, and to help me serve those I may have wronged."[60] Harold said that it is hard for men to "loosen their grip because they focus too much on the self." Don added that men often "serve another master," such as money or prestige.

Joseph entered the discussion by talking about homeschooling his children as an attempt to get his house in order. He then talked about why they were homeschooling in the first place – because of what is going on in the public schools and the values that are promoted or condoned there. Joseph stated, with some hesitation, "Well, they even have a lesbian gym teacher." Harold quickly added "That's where you'll find them, hanging around children and in athletics." No one disagreed. Joseph's statement was uttered with a degree of disbelief; Harold's was not.

It is not always clear what the group's position is when someone makes a general statement such as Harold's "That's where you'll find them." The lack of disagreement cannot be assumed to be general agreement. It could mean acceptance, insecurity about one's own opinion, an effort to avoid confrontation, or perhaps embarrassment. The men do contest each other at certain times. Once, Joseph said that women have taken over the leadership of the family; he implied that women were to blame for the disintegration of traditional family values. Almost in unison, the group challenged him, upholding the view usually stated by Promise Keepers that women have only stepped into the leadership role because men have abdicated it. Men have failed, the others emphasized, women have only taken on more responsibility because of men's failures.

The group then read Luke 18:18-27 to start the next lesson. The lesson is titled "So, What's Wrong With Being Rich?" It is described as an effort to shed insight on Promise 1: A Man and his God. Luke 18:18-27 is a story about a rich man who wants to inherit eternal life. Jesus tells the rich man that he must follow the commandments of the Bible, specifically listing the commandments against adultery, murder, theft and giving false testimony, and the commandment to honor one's father and mother. The rich man replies that he has honored all the commandments. Jesus then tells the rich man that he must also "Sell everything you have and give to the poor, and you will have treasure in heaven. Then come, follow me."[61]This passage is then followed by a familiar passage to the men: "Indeed, it is easier for a camel to go through the eye of a needle than for a rich man to enter the kingdom of God".[62]

This led to a discussion of the problems associated with being a Christian and rich. They discussed the recently publicized offer of 30 million dollars over five years to Phil Jackson, the coach of the Chicago Bulls, to lead a competing team. Joseph said he would take Jackson's job for only one million a year; Harold joked he would take a million dollars just once in his lifetime.

On a more serious note, Harold said he likes his lifestyle just the way it is, by "modest means" as he described his way of living. Lottery winners were mentioned as a common example of people who come into money and it begins to change their lives. Harold said that people generally "reward the Lord by forgetting him when they become rich." Ed added that "they forget to praise the Lord for their good fortune and the money cannot provide eternal life, only the Lord can do that."

The lottery is an easy example for the men to discuss because it privileges the individual fortunate enough to purchase a winning lottery ticket. The lottery minimizes individual ability to pure chance, which is easily seen as the Lord's grace. It is much more difficult for them to discuss the self-made man in the context of becoming wealthy.

Harold and I cleaned up while the others left for work. Harold said that "We (men) have let our children down and Promise Keepers makes you aware of this fact. These morning discussions make men aware of different ideas." He described them as "thought provoking hours with biblical guidance; a place where Bible meets culture." Harold said he thought it was a good idea to provoke men to make them think about what they are doing. This is the first time Harold has ever been involved in a men's group. He credits Promise Keepers for making this happen.

At another men's small group I attended, the group dynamics were more focused on biblical study than fellowship and prayer. The "United Faith" group involves three white men, all of relatively the same age and social class. They began the session with some fellowship, followed by a prayer and Bible study. The men do not join hands while praying, preferring to bow their heads individually and clasp their own hands. On the day I visited, the men did not sing any songs of praise.

The men sat around a large conference table, an empty chair between each man. The group's main focus was biblical study. They were analytical and showed little emotion as compared to the New Bethel group. The Saturday morning when I visited the group they discussed Esther 4:1-17.

Bob expressed empathy for Esther's plight. Esther is being urged to stand up for the Jews and their religion in the face of persecution by Hammon, the military deputy of King Xerxes. In the passages studied, Mordecai urges her to tell the King of Hammon's evil intentions, thereby putting herself in danger and admitting to Xerxes that she is a Jew.

Bob admitted that he has a similar problem as Esther's; he does not tell the people with whom he works that he is a born-again Christian. Bob said he was saved last year at the Chicago Promise Keepers stadium conference at Soldiers Field. Before the conference he did not know the Lord, spent his Sundays playing baseball, and had a failing marriage and an unfulfilled life. He told me that he was saved at the Friday night altar call held at every Promise Keepers stadium conference. Bob said he stayed in his seat almost the whole weekend, leaving only for lunch and restroom breaks. He sat in his seat and reflected on his life and how he wanted to commit his life to Christ. In the year since the stadium event, Bob has studied scripture and joined two men's groups. He credits Promise Keepers with changing his life at home and at work.

But he still wonders how much to witness to others about his relationship with Christ. He is worried about a particular client at work who only knows the "old" Bob. The client has a habit of poking fun at born-again Christians. The two men share a common friend who is a Jehovah's Witness. The client ridicules this man for going door to door in order to witness to strangers. According to Bob, the client thinks of himself as a Christian, but Bob doubts the man's sincerity. Bob asked the group how he should proceed, admitting he did not think he had the courage of Esther.

Kevin recommended that Bob bide his time and wait for an appropriate moment. He said that when he faces similar situations he waits for the Lord to "lay it on my heart."

To "lay it on my heart" is a phrase used by Kevin (and other Promise Keepers) to describe how the Lord works in his life. He told a story about bedtime prayer with his daughter. On a recent evening they spent almost twenty minutes going through various prayer requests his daughter had mentioned; issues that were laying on her heart. The daughter would mention and/or describe a situation and then Kevin would lead her in prayer. Kevin said his daughter wanted to pray for Paula Jones and President Clinton. Jones' sexual harassment case against President Clinton had just been addressed by the Supreme Court. The court ruled that the case could proceed, thus placing the President in an awkward situation. Kevin's daughter wanted to pray for a resolution to the case, but wondered why the President had not apologized to Paula Jones. Kevin told his daughter that the President does not apologize because he does not think he has done anything wrong. The daughter responded that Paula Jones thinks he did something wrong, so he should apologize anyway since he is a Christian.

Bob responded that he did not think President Clinton was much of a Christian. Kevin added that the President claims to pray for guidance all the time. With that in mind, Bob quipped, he might have to start listening to him once in awhile. This brought about some light laughter.

Similar to the New Bethel group, this group also exhibits signs of being antipolitical rather than apolitical. Politics is that which is avoided; it is something to be deflected with humor.

Returning to Bob's question, John, the third member of the group, said that he just avoids such situations. His office is terrible for having un-Christian attitudes, so he now spends 95 percent of his time out of the office, either working at home or with clients. This led to a specific discussion of Esther 4:14:

> For if you remain silent at this time, relief and deliverance for the Jews will arise from another place, but you and your father's family will perish. And who knows but that you have come to royal position for such a time as this?

Bob termed this passage "the kicker." Everyone agreed that the last sentence in the passage was very profound since you never really know when you may have a lasting effect on someone. Bob said he remembered a quote stating that one negative observation can erase the benefit of ten positive experiences. John said that many people are told at a young age that they are no good at something, for example, singing, and then 30 years later they still believe the statement. Bob described how each time he deals with his children he tries to remember that everything he does and says may have a profound and lasting impact on them.

Kevin concurred and added that perhaps that was why they were gathered together. Bill McCartney, the founder of Promise Keepers, did not know that his position in life would end up affecting so many lives. Kevin described how Promise Keepers began from a simple conversation between two men riding in a car and how it was developed through a small group of men meeting together in prayer and fellowship. Kevin credits such simple origins with bringing him closer to Christ and for his becoming involved in two men's accountability groups.

Bob, a salesman with a flair for the dramatic, posed interesting and thoughtful questions and scenarios. He constructed a situation in which a man would confront him in his office and tell him that if he did not deny Jesus Christ and the truth of the Bible, then he would be shot instantly. His options were to deny Christ or to be killed. Bob was not sure what he would do in such a situation. He wanted to believe he would never deny his Savior, but he also acknowledged his pragmatic side. He noted that there were several occasions in the Bible in which Christians had denied Christ in order to spare their lives to work for Christ at a later date.

Kevin said he hoped that he would have the strength to stand up for Christ, even if it would mean the end of his life on earth. He was consoled by the fact that it would only be the end of his physical life and not his spiritual one. He said that three years ago, prior to his involvement with Promise Keepers, he would not have been able to make such a commitment. He would have perceived such a sacrificial stand to be absurd. But today, he prays for the courage to stand up for his convictions and for the Lord. He said that this form of persecution is actually taking place around the world. He mentioned a recent program he had heard on James Dobson's Focus on the Family describing how Christians were being persecuted for their beliefs in many Third World countries.

Kevin then expanded his story to include the group dynamic so often relied on by Promise Keepers. He said if they, the three of them, were in a church and some armed men broke into the church and demanded that they stop worshiping their God and renounce Christ by spitting on his image as they left the church, that it would be hard to follow such orders if both Bob and John refused to spit on the image of Christ as they left the sanctuary. But if they renounced Christ, it would be very difficult for him to stand alone. Kevin said that is why Promise

Keepers is so important; it asks men to stand together and not try to stand alone. Promise Keepers encourages and recommends vital relationships between Christian men because men are constantly tempted by a culture that dismisses their beliefs. According to Kevin, contemporary culture often makes the same demands as the armed men storming the church. Men trying to stand alone will fail; men standing together and supporting each other have the potential to stand up for what they believe.

## Concluding Thought

In one of the observed group discussions, Walter told the men about his childhood impressions of Bob Kennedy. More than thirty years ago, in Gary, Indiana, Walter remembers the hope his family had in a political solution to the problems they were facing. Walter was told that Bobby Kennedy was going to be their savior, that he was going to help the black community and solve the problems of the inner city. According to Walter, the help never materialized. Not because of any assassin's bullet, but because people were looking in the wrong place for salvation. Today, Walter believes the answer lies in turning one's attention to the Lord rather than the government. Governments come and go, but, according to Walter, the Lord is always there for the believer.

## Notes

1. Louis Althusser, "Ideology and Ideological State Apparatuses," in *Lenin and Philosophy and other essays,* trans. Ben Brewster (New York: Monthly Review, 1971), 127-186. Interpellation is similar to the concept of socialization. Both describe how an individual lives in society. The subtle difference is that socialization generally focuses on adapting the individual to the needs of society, whereas interpellation also discerns the subject positions (identities) that an individual is hailed into accepting/performing. Take for example the person who answers a ringing phone. Socialization tells me the rules and customs expected of someone who answers a phone – a greeting followed by the need to talk. Interpellation highlights the process of hailing – do I become a friend, brother, husband, son, or subject of some telemarketer's script, which is then followed by rules of socialization. But in the moment of answering the hail of the ringing telephone is the interpellation, we become a particular subject. In the case of the "do you know the Lord" question, Bill was hailing me (the ringing phone) to become a subject (a specific Bryan) in relation to Christianity.

Althusser describes it in the following manner:

> I shall then suggest that ideology 'acts' or 'functions' in such a way that it 'recruits' subjects among the individuals (it recruits them all), or 'transforms' the individuals into subjects (it transforms them all) by that very precise operation which I have called *interpellation* or hailing, and which can be imagined along the lines of the most commonplace everyday police (or other) hailing: 'Hey, you there!' (174)

2. See also Robert Booth Fowler and Allen D. Hertzke, *Religion and Politics in America: Faith, Culture, and Strategic Choices* (Boulder, CO: Westview Press, 1995), 37.

3. Kip Burke, "Promise Keepers Calls Men to 'Stand in the Gap,'" *New Man*, (March-April 1997), 21.

4. Tony Evans, "Spiritual Purity," in *Seven Promises of a Promise Keeper,* ed. Al Janssen (Colorado Springs: Focus on the Family Publishing, 1994), 79.

5. Charles W. Colson, "A Man and His Integrity," in *Go the Distance*, ed. John Trent (Colorado Springs: Focus on the Family Publishing, 1996), 112.

6. *New Man* interview with Raleigh Washington, "Wall Busting 101" (September 1996), 39.

7. Bill McCartney, Letter to conference attendees, Promise Keepers Homepage, promisekeepers.org (Summer 1997).

8. Promise Keepers Statement of Faith.

9. Promise Keepers Conference Program 1996, 19.

10. Promise Keepers Ambassador Training 1995, 9.

11. For a discussion of *bricolage* see Deena Weinstein and Michael A Weinstein, *Postmodern(ized) Simmel* (London: Routledge, 1993), 62-70.

12. Catharine A. MacKinnon, *Toward a Feminist Theory of the State* (Cambridge, MA: Harvard University Press, 1989), 83.

13. Ibid., 83.

14. Jane De Hart Mathews, "The New Feminism and the Dynamics of Social Change," in *Women's America: Refocusing the Past,* ed. Linda K. Kerber and Jane De Hart Mathews (New York: Oxford University Press, 1982), 412.

15. *Seven Promises of a Promise Keeper,* ed. Al Janssen (Colorado Springs: Focus on the Family Publishing, 1994), 43.

16. Promise Keepers Homepage, "Meet Jesus," promisekeepers.org (Summer 1997), 6.

17. Geoff Gorsuch, with Dan Schaffer, *BROTHERS! Calling Men Into Vital Relationships: A Small Group Discussion Guide* (Colorado Springs: NavPress, 1994), 22. See also Robert Hicks, *Uneasy Manhood* (Nashville: Oliver-Nelson, 1991), 52.

18. Rodney L. Cooper, *Double Bind: Escaping the Contradictory Demands of Manhood* (Grand Rapids, MI: Zondervan Publishing House, 1996), 7-18.

19. MacKinnon, *Toward a Feminist Theory of the State*, 84.

20. Ibid., 84.

21. Ibid., 84.

22. Promise Keepers Men's Conference Program 1996, 8.

23. MacKinnon, *Toward a Feminist Theory of the State,* 86.

24. Promise Keepers Men's Conference Program 1996, 28.

25. MacKinnon, *Toward a Feminist Theory of the State,* 86.

26. Pete Richardson, *Focusing Your Men's Ministry: A Strategy for Layleaders and Pastors* (Boulder, CO: Promise Keepers, 1993), 19.

27. Ibid., 20.

28. Simone de Beauvoir, *The Second Sex* (New York: Vintage Books, 1989), xxiii. (Original work published 1952.)

29. Ibid., xxi.

30. Judith Butler, *Bodies That Matter: On the Discursive Limits of "Sex"* (New York: Routledge, 1993), 94.

31. Ibid., 94.

32. Promise Keepers Men's Conference Brochure 1997, 12.

33. Promise Keepers Men's Conference Brochure 1997, 14.

34. Full passage of Ephesians 2:12-13; [12]remember that at that time you were separate from Christ, excluded from citizenship in Israel and foreigners to the covenants of the promise, without hope and without God in the world. [13]But now in Christ Jesus you who once were far away have been brought near through the blood of Christ.

35. Promise Keepers, *Man of His Word Bible*, 1.

36. Ibid. A removable card inside the front cover.

37. Promise Keepers Men's Conference Brochure, *The Making of a Godly Man.* (1997), 52.

38. Pete Richardson, *Focusing Your Men's Ministry*, 9.

39. Bob Horner, Ron Ralston, and David Sunde, *Promise Builders Study Series: Applying the Seven Promises* (Colorado Springs: Focus on the Family Publishing, 1996), 11.

40. Ibid., 8.

41. Ibid., 8.

42. Ibid., 8-9.

43. Ibid., 7.

44. Ibid., 7.

45. Michel Foucault, *The Archaeology of Knowledge & The Discourse on Language*, trans. A.M. Sheridan Smith (New York: Pantheon Books, 1972), 49.

46. Geoff Gorsuch, *BROTHERS!*, 31.

47. Ibid., 34.

48. Ibid., 34.

49. Ibid., 40.

50. Foucault, *The Archaeology of Knowledge*, 51.

51. Gorsuch, *BROTHERS!*, 45.

52. Ibid., 50-51.

53. Ibid., 50.

54. Foucault, *The Archaeology of Knowledge*, 52.

55. Gorsuch, *BROTHERS!*, 56.

56. Ibid., 56.

57. Foucault, *The Archaeology of Knowledge*, 55.

58. Ibid., 55.

59. Horner, Ralston, Sunde, *Promise Builders Study Series*, 55.

60. Ibid., 55.

61. Luke 18:22.

62. Luke 18:25.

# Chapter Two

---

## Building an Evangelical Organization: The Lincoln Bedroom or Oval Office Model?

In many ways, ostensibly beginning with Jimmy Carter's election in 1976 and his declaration of being a born-again Christian, evangelicalism has played an influential role in contemporary American politics and culture. Historically, evangelicals had shunned the political realm. Politics was viewed as "an engagement with the sinful world God meant" them to eschew.[1] But, with Carter's election, the rise of Jerry Falwell's Moral Majority during the 1980s, and Pat Robertson's 1988 presidential campaign, the relation of an evangelical to politics has been transformed.[2]

Evangelicals are a diverse category of Christians who commonly accept three basic tenets, but who vary on the tactical implementation of one tenet. The three basic tenets that define an evangelical are conversion, biblicism, and activism.[3] Conversion, being born-again, and biblicism, a respectful and literal interpretation of the Bible, foster little debate among evangelicals. It is the interpretation of the third defining characteristic, activism, that often differentiates what I will refer to as "traditional" and "new" evangelicals.

Traditional evangelicals, epitomized by Billy Graham, emphasize "personal conversion and mass evangelism."[4] New evangelicals, epitomized in the 1970s by Jerry Falwell and recently by Pat Robertson, also emphasize personal conversion and mass evangelism but stress the political import of faith. Within the two categories there are other important characteristics, such as the degree of fundamentalism (how strictly one interprets the Bible), charismatic worship (glossolalia, healing, contemporary music, intense group experiences), and ecumenism. While all three aspects are important to an understanding of evangelicalism in general, none affect the potential political mobilization of evangelicals as much as the way in which they relate to the tenet of activism.

Typically, but with varying degrees of fervor, evangelicals portray secular (liberal) society as chaotic while also calling for a return to a more traditional, that is, biblical, moral order. Traditional, or "mainstream" evangelicals,[5] in the tradition of Billy Graham, focus their activism primarily on the individual experience of regeneration and little, if at all, on the negative implications of a liberal social order. New evangelicals, however, advocate involvement in the political system to combat the influence of secular humanism. Both the traditional and new evangelicals are committed to the great commission, to spread the good news (evangelism), but they differ on tactical implementation. Both the traditional and new evangelicals focus on conversion, biblicism, and activism, but only new evangelicals attempt to use activism to affect the political process.

A metaphor: traditional evangelicals evangelize and may one day influence the social order to the degree that they may be invited to the White House to sleep in the Lincoln Bedroom (Billy Graham); new evangelicals may also be invited to sleep in the Lincoln Bedroom, but they also harbor aspirations for the power of the Oval Office (Pat Robertson).

The question concerning an analysis of the Promise Keepers is where do they fit into the evangelical spectrum: traditional or new? Are they, metaphorically, potentially bedroom guests, Oval Office occupants, or something else? In other words, are the men involved in Promise Keepers, at both the leadership and local level, part of a new "crypto-Religious Right" movement, as they have been accused of being,[6] part of the traditional antipolitical strain of evangelicalism, or rather, are the Promise Keepers the product of a new form of evangelicalism?

By "crypto-Religious Right," I refer to Promise Keepers' well known claim to be an apolitical organization. Many social and political commentators have questioned the integrity of this position and have characterized the Promise Keepers as a Trojan Horse of the Religious Right.

This is both true and false. As I argued in the previous chapter, the men involved in Promise Keepers at the local level and who attend the stadium conferences are generally antipolitical. They are evangelicals, but more aptly characterized after the work of Billy Graham. On the other hand, the men leading Promise Keepers (founder, president, board members, conference speakers, and boosters) are a mix of traditional and new evangelicals. The remainder of this chapter attempts to distill the traditional from the new. The following sections discuss the similarities between building and coaching the University of Colorado's football team and founding and enacting the evangelical vision for Promise Keepers, the "spawning" of PK from Vineyard, and the various aspects that support and are incorporated into a "championship" team, including boosters, players, public relations, and team goals.

## Coach McCartney and PK McCartney

As iron sharpens iron, so one man sharpens another.
Proverbs 27:17

What does not destroy me, strengthens me.
- Nietzsche
Epigraph in Bill McCartney's autobiography, *From Ashes to Glory*

Bill McCartney, cofounder and CEO of Promise Keepers, is the excoach of the University of Colorado's football team. His autobiography, *From Ashes to Glory*, combines his growth as a football coach with the development of his spiritual relationship with Jesus Christ. The book weaves one of McCartney's passions, football, into his life long walk (search) for Christ-likeness, defined as spiritual growth and maturity in the image of Christ.

The epigraph to this section that was taken from Nietzsche is the leading epigraph to a chapter in McCartney's autobiography. The chapter, titled "My Personal Cross," is the only one in the book beginning with an epigraph and, not surprisingly, the only place Nietzsche is mentioned. The quote made me wonder why Nietzsche, the self proclaimed Anti-Christ, was providing philosophical instruction to McCartney's life story, particularly concerning the burden of his cross.

In the chapter it becomes clear why Nietzsche's words were used to introduce the passage. McCartney views life, football, and spiritual growth as a confrontation with potentially destructive forces, which, if survived, can be used to build one's character. For Coach McCartney, football is a struggle between opposing teams. Promise Keeper McCartney understands spiritual growth to be a struggle between opposing forces, one Good, the other Evil. In both scenarios, one's character is forged by enduring and learning from one's trials and tribulations. And, as the successful coach of a team sport, McCartney knows the value of enduring life's battles with the support of teammates, thus the significance of Proverbs 27:17, a commonly cited Scripture in the Promise Keepers organization: "As iron sharpens iron, so one man sharpens another."

Coach McCartney, the man who rebuilt the University of Colorado football program and led it to a national championship, is not unlike Promise Keeper McCartney. The evangelizing McCartney encourages men to commit to Jesus Christ instead of the University of Colorado's football team, but in both cases, it is in order to lead the group to a championship season.

In *From Ashes to Glory*, and more recently in *Sold Out*, Coach McCartney details how he and others (staff, players, boosters, and University officials) rebuilt the Colorado football program. McCartney readily acknowledges that winning football programs are not built through the efforts of one man. He stresses the principles that, in a team sport, championships are never won alone and champions are never made in isolation. McCartney believes that every organization needs leadership and goals; a group needs to understand what it is working toward and how it is going to get there.

According to McCartney, when he arrived in Boulder, the football program was lacking direction. It lacked talent, organization, motivation, and, most importantly, team goals. McCartney gave the program direction. He brought focus to an unorganized team and instilled a standard of excellence. Part of the standard of excellence was built upon the image of the Nebraska football team, the team the Buffaloes most wanted to defeat. The game against Nebraska became the touchstone for measuring success. The Nebraska football team provided Colorado two things – a program to be modeled and an enemy to be defeated.

But coaching football used to be McCartney's passion; bringing men into a relationship with Christ is McCartney's new passion. The two are not altogether different. The same leadership principles, organizational skills, strategic thinking, relationship building (i.e., recruiting and teaching), and competitive attitude that made him a successful coach have also contributed to the amazing growth of the Promise Keepers organization.

Researching McCartney through the role of a coach, a role he describes as being a "motivator, manager, and defender,"[7] also gives one insight into the language he uses. Football coaches often use the language of combat to motivate players, "the line of scrimmage," "in the trenches," "it's war out there!" When McCartney wrote (to other Promise Keepers) that "We're in a war, men, whether we acknowledge it or not. The enemy is real and he doesn't like to see men of God take a stand for Jesus Christ and contest his lies,"[8] it is the football coach turned pulpit layman, the coach as motivator.

As motivator and defender, McCartney has called Promise Keepers to rally together in order to battle a common foe and to help their fellow man (teammate):

> We have a unique opportunity today, the chance to stand up, be counted, and give men who have chosen a different road an alternative before it's too late. We need to recapture the spiritual climate in our own homes and cultivate a heart for other men. Our homes, men, are about to collapse. The homes we live in are coming apart at the seams. But we can't just worry about our own homes. We've got to foster regard and concern for the homes around us. Together we must stand up and be counted for Almighty God.[9]

Promise Keeper McCartney manages the organization the same way he guided the Colorado football team. A coach knows that in order to manage, one must be able to communicate a vision, particularly the team concept. A coach also knows that most improvement comes from practice and training performed during the off-season, a time when a coach has little direct contact with his or her players. In order to manage an individual's development, coaches use various forms of communication. While at Colorado, McCartney would write letters to his players in order to motivate them during the summer prior to the start of training camp in August. The following is an excerpt from a letter that McCartney wrote to his players in the summer of 1988 on the meaning and importance of becoming a team;

> A legitimate team member is loyal. This means he is committed to each player and coach twenty-four hours a day. He respects each guy regardless of class, culture, creed, or color. He defends each man behind closed doors or in public view. He refuses to put down or slander his teammate under any circumstances. He allows for differences and always gives his teammate the benefit of the doubt. He offers an opinion about a teammate only when it presents a positive and supportive posture. If he has offended a teammate, he willingly goes to him and resolves the problem.[10]

The intent of the letter was captured in McCartney's autobiography when he follows these words with his own observation: "Only by coming together completely as a team could we generate the power to conquer."[11]

In order to win football games, McCartney understood that a coach must harness a player's ability and train each individual to perform within a cohesive unit. A coach needs the team to be unified, to be self-less, to respect each other, and to have a fulltime commitment to the team goals in order to "generate the power to conquer."

According to McCartney, the same team effort is needed in order for Promise Keepers to generate the power to succeed. Compare Coach McCartney's letter to his football players in 1988 to the words of PK McCartney as he encouraged men to prepare for the 1997 Stand in the Gap assembly in Washington, D.C. The following excerpt is taken from the introduction to a 40-day prayer journal written by McCartney and sent to men who registered for the assembly. Just as Coach McCartney would prepare the players for the upcoming season, PK McCartney is encouraging Christian men during the "off-season" for the upcoming season of revival:

> When I was at Colorado, the Buff's arch rival was Nebraska. We'd travel to Lincoln knowing Cornhusker Stadium would be an explosive, hostile environment. Because it was such a tough place to play, we made every preparation to block out the noise, the angry crowd, the in-your-face intimidation. Men, I'm telling you that Washington, DC, is a tough place to play. God's sacred assembly will be met with great hostility. The spiritual opposition will be intense and ugly. If men show up with whimsical expectations, unwitting and unprepared, they're going to get blindsided. And if that happens, Stand In The Gap will be little more than [a] one-day event creating some excitement – the airlines and Washington hotels will be pleased – but its impact will soon fade. That's why there must be deep preceding preparation in men's hearts. What if a multitude of men began disciplining themselves to pray, personally and in small groups, and began to practice a lifestyle of confession and repentance? What if a multitude of men committed themselves to know Him, and to cleanse their lives of sin? Would it please God to answer their prayers for revival?[12]

Promise Keeper McCartney sees a civil society led astray by false values ("We exist in a sinful world occupied by hedonistic people whose god is the almighty dollar"),[13] a typical evangelical perspective, and a situation similar to the misguided team he found in Boulder upon his arrival in 1982. McCartney believes good players will compete if given the proper conditioning, training, and coaching. He also believes in the ability of "strong men to lead weak men."[14] Reading Bill McCartney as the motivator, manager, and defender of the Promise Keepers team is a way to understand the movement's presentation and its appeal to a multitude of men.

## The Organization

Promise Keepers is headquartered in Denver, Colorado, but the strength of the organization comes from its national ministries. PK serves men through conferences and educational and field ministries as well as through the development of Christian resources. In 1997 Promise Keepers had eight state and regional offices, which were supported by a total of 59 Area Managers, that provided information to and organized training in specific regions.

According to Promise Keepers:

> The National Field Ministries Division of Promise Keepers exists to carry the vision and mission of the ministry to the grass roots of its constituency; building an effective team to recruit, train, and deploy men who have a passion for the local church, for revival and for effective ministry of men, thus facilitating the keeping of promises.[15]

To facilitate helping men keep their promises in local men's ministry, PK organizes and trains what they refer to as Key Men. A Key Man is described as a man who should be:

1. A leader and/or facilitator of the men's ministry in his local church.

2. Part of a team which serves as a strategic link between the local congregation and Promise Keepers, under the guidance of his pastor.

3. Committed to building an environment where men grow in their relationship with Jesus Christ and each other.[16]

Key Men work in their local church to foster an environment that is comfortable to men, what PK refers to as the "male context." Promise Keepers believes that "men's groups are successful when structured in such a way that they work with the unique way God made men," the male context.[17] The male context is based on six principles that are "unique" to men, such as "men, in general, view space as safety and closeness or intimacy as a threat" and that men tend to express all their emotions "as anger or a sexual response."[18] With the acceptance of negative stereotypes of males, the Key Man is trained to overcome the pitfalls that have plagued previous men's ministries by developing a male context within his church.

A Key Man is supported by a volunteer representative of Promise Keepers called an Ambassador. The Ambassador represents Promise Keepers to a group of assigned churches in a given area.[19] The following list describes the role of an Ambassador:

1. Communicates the mission of Promise Keepers and identifies Key Men with the aid of the local pastor.

2. Relational networking: He has moved beyond making contacts to developing a relational network.

3. Encouraging his Key Men as a top priority.

4. Resources Key Men, exchanges ideas and information to help facilitate the task of his Key Men.[20]

As Ambassadors work to support Key Men, they are in turn supported by a state or regional Task Force. Each Task Force is composed of "six to 15 men who work closely with Promise Keepers state and regional offices" to develop strategy and coordinate resources.[21] The Task Force meets regularly to do the following:

1. Coordinate efforts to reach out to churches in their community

2. Manage the logistics for Key Man and Ambassador training

3. Coordinate events and other training seminars with their community

4. Build momentum for conferences

5. Carry out other responsibilities as directed by the Promise Keepers field staff

Promise Keepers field ministries, training and utilization of Key Men and Ambassadors develops the leaders necessary for a national organization to disseminate its message. With the team concept in mind, the organizational structure is designed to support the local men's ministry with educational resources and organizational training that facilitate the "construction" of a male friendly environment within the church, thus bringing men (back) into a relationship with Christ.

*The Promise Keepers Team*

A well run organization understands its mission. When new members join an organization, a statement detailing what the organization stands for is necessary to foster cohesion. The Seven Promises of a Promise Keeper are probably the best known example of what a Promise Keeper is committed to fulfill. But the promises, which are discussed in more detail in the following chapter, are aimed at the personal integrity of each individual man, each team player if you will. The organization, made up of men already committed to the Seven Promises, requires biblical principles for guidance. These principles are listed in the Promise Keepers Statement of Faith:

1. We believe that there is one God eternally existing in three persons: the Father, the Son, and the Holy Spirit.

2. We believe that the Bible is God's written revelation to man and that it is verbally inspired, authoritative, and without error in the original manuscript.

3. We believe in the deity of Jesus Christ, His virgin birth, sinless life, miracles, death on the cross to provide for our redemption, bodily resurrection and ascension into heaven, present ministry of intercession for us, and His return to earth in power and glory.

4. We believe in the personality and deity of the Holy Spirit, that He performs the miracle of new birth in an unbeliever and indwells believers, enabling them to live a godly life.

5. We believe that man was created in the image of God, but because of sin, was alienated from God. That alienation can be removed only by accepting through faith alone God's gift of salvation which was made possible by Christ's death.[22]

The Promise Keepers Statement of Faith locates the movement within contemporary evangelical Christianity.[23] The statement of faith distinguishes the Promise Keepers from recent liberal interpretations of Christian theology, in particular, their belief in the Bible as "without error in the original manuscript" (biblicism). Two points should be noted in this regard. First, to claim that the Bible is without error in the original manuscript does not eliminate the need to interpret the Bible. As I will argue below, well intentioned and sincere Christians often differ on the meaning of Scripture. The most accurate critiques of the Promise Keepers originate from other Christian organizations concerning their interpretation of Scripture.

Second, the Promise Keepers believe that the Holy Spirit lives (indwells) in believers (born-again, conversion). They are never alone; the Spirit is always with them. This makes Promise Keepers different from mainstream Christians in feeling if not in faith. All Christians have a relationship with the holy trinity, but Promise Keepers are supposed to see the trinity in all that they experience.

*Team Goals and Reconciliation*

Every team has goals. Goals organize and focus the efforts and will of the team. For the Promise Keepers, the goals are summarized and outlined in the Seven Promises of a Promise Keeper (Appendix). A characteristic of all the promises, and a fundamental goal of Promise Keepers, is an attempt to promote reconciliation. Reconciliation is how one comes to terms with an object, be it God, Christ, sin, marriage, or a brother. A Promise Keeper is called to reconcile his lived perspective to the experienced world as God's will (PK refers to 2 Corinthians 5:18-20). His happiness and melancholy, joy and sorrow, his feelings of sacred and profane things, are all part of his walk with Christ and can be reconciled to God's will. Rather than accepting the hail (interpellation) of a man thrown to the world to fend for himself, of one stumbling toward the abyss, the Promise Keeper reconciles his experiences to God's way.

Reconciliation also distinguishes Promise Keepers from either traditional or new evangelicalism. The Promise Keepers ideology broadens traditional evangelicalism and limits new evangelicalism to form what I will refer to as "social evangelicalism." Social evangelicalism maintains the importance of personal faith but is not inclined to political action. Social evangelicalism focuses on social relationships. Bill McCartney explains:

> In my mind, Promise Keepers is really a ministry of reconciliation. We want to help men heal the lost and broken relationships in their lives. We want to see fathers and sons reunited in love and repentance. We want to see men reconcile with their wives and recommit to their marriage relationships. And we want to see men fall down before God and repent of their past sins – whether sins of immorality or sins of apathy – and pledge to turn the tide and do better. I truly believe that there is not a single wound that cannot be healed, nor a single heart that cannot be softened, through the love of Jesus Christ.[24]

Reconciliation stands in for, and/or palliates, sacrifice, what Nietzsche called the religious or sacrificial nature.[25] Reconciliation binds one's life to a relationship with an other. The Promise Keepers focus on social reconciliation is a new variant of evangelicalism. Whereas traditional evangelicals (as well as PK) foster reconciliation between an individual and God, and new evangelicals promote the reconciliation of politics to God's way, Promise Keepers, as social evangelicals, promote reconciliation of a man's relationship with God, his wife, children, family, friends, and coworkers.

The issue of reconciliation also differs from redemption, but the two are closely connected. Redemption gives meaning to all acts; reconciliation binds one to the doing, positing (interpellating) the doer into a relationship with the deed, whether actual or vicarious. No relationship is lost or sacrificed without meaning. As a team goal, reconciliation, the palliation of sacrifice, elicits empathy for one's predicament through God's will. Reconciliation not only gives meaning to one's life (redemption), but it also binds one's relationship to the Father, Son, and Holy Spirit.

## PK Team Members, Speakers, and Board Members

The men who lead the Promise Keepers team bring to the movement diverse backgrounds, success in founding and leading other Christian evangelical organizations, and an unyielding belief in ecumenism. According to Gabriel Fackre, author of *Ecumenical Faith in Evangelical Perspective*, ecumenism is "more of a tendency than a constituency" among evangelicals.[26] Ecumenism is the belief in a unified Christian church divested of any particular denomination's doctrinal concerns. Similarly to other Christian ideologies, ecumenism holds the belief in Jesus Christ to be the most significant tenet of Christianity. But how one comes to know Jesus, worship him, and obey his word, are of less importance; for ecumenists, worshiping Christ is the fundamental concern.

*James Ryle and the Vineyard*

One of the men involved in the leadership of Promise Keepers is James Ryle, Senior Pastor at Vineyard Christian Fellowship Boulder Valley, located in Longmont, CO. Boulder Valley is also the church attended by Bill McCartney and Promise Keepers President Randy Phillips. Ryle is a conference speaker and board member for Promise Keepers. He was the team Chaplain for the University of Colorado football team while Bill McCartney was the team's coach. Ryle is the author of *Hippo in the Garden* and *A Dream Come True*. Both books deal with the individual's ability to perceive, interpret, and enact God's guidance in their daily life.

Ryle stated in an interview with *Gentlemen's Quarterly* writer Scott Raab that "Nothing in the world, . . . could have ever possibly happened worse, in the whole world, than for Promise Keepers – this incredible, significant, undeniably noble movement – to have been spawned out of the Vineyard."[27] Ryle's concern regarding the spawning of Promise Keepers comes from the fact that the Vineyard movement is considered a radical (heretical) understanding of Christian theology.[28]

The Vineyard Christian Fellowship Boulder Valley Homepage has a section listing the beliefs of the church. Part of the "What Do We Believe?" section states the following:

> We believe the Holy Spirit indwells every believer in Jesus Christ and that He is an abiding helper, teacher and guide. We believe in the present ministry of the Holy Spirit and in the exercise of all biblical gifts of the Spirit.[29]

At least two parts of this statement require analysis in order to distinguish Vineyard from other forms of Christianity. The first part, concerning the work of the Holy Spirit as it indwells every believer of Jesus Christ, clearly places the Vineyard in the category of born-again Christianity. But, as will be discussed below, the suspected influence of Vineyard theology on the leadership of Promise Keepers, is a pressing concern to many traditional Christians. The idea that the Holy Spirit is an "abiding helper, teacher and guide" is widely accepted within Christianity. It is the "exercise of all biblical gifts of the Spirit" that concerns Christian critics. If the Holy Spirit is an abiding helper, teacher, and guide, then it would be in the interest of all Christians to get in touch with God through the Spirit. Ryle believes that God speaks to individuals through dreams and visions, extra-biblical revelations affecting every day life. His point, and that of Vineyard ministries, is that individuals have forgotten or lost the ability to understand their lives in light of God's attempts to communicate with them. Ryle believes Christians must "get past the barriers of unbelief" and begin listening to God's word in their daily life.[30]

Ryle is an important person in McCartney's spiritual growth. Prior to attending Ryle's church in Boulder, McCartney claimed to be a born-again Catholic.[31] In June of 1989, McCartney attended Ryle's Vineyard church for the first time and has been associated with the ministry ever since. The belief in modern day prophesies distinguishes Vineyard ministries from mainstream Christianity, since it fosters and encourages prophetic communications from God through the Holy Spirit. This is an important influence of the group since all three men (Ryle, McCartney, and Phillips) use phrases such as 'dream' and 'vision' to describe their beliefs and God's influence.

McCartney credits Ryle with prophesying in August of 1989 the University of Colorado football team's "Golden Season," in which the team was 10-0 until losing to Notre Dame in the 1990 Orange Bowl.[32] McCartney and his wife first attended Ryle's Vineyard church on June 25, 1989. Less than two months later, McCartney describes in his autobiography how Pastor Ryle showed up at football practice and told him about his dream:

> On August 22, he (Ryle) showed up at practice and motioned that we needed to talk. I joined him at the sideline, where he proceeded to tell me that he'd had a dream. More than a dream, really. He said it was something God wanted me to know.
>
> This is precisely the way he related it to me:
>
> In a dream I saw the Colorado University football team kneeling in a huddle on the playing field, with a dark cloud pressing down upon them. The situation seemed oppressive and hopeless. Then suddenly, what seemed like the hand of God came forth and swept the cloud away with one quick, decisive, and unchallenged stroke.
>
> A rainbow then appeared and penetrated into the center of the huddle. The players were wearing black jerseys and gold helmets, making the scene literally look like a pot of gold at the end of the rainbow. The light of the rainbow

> caused the gold helmets to become brilliant, having a radiant glow like pure gold under bright lights. Simultaneously, I saw what appeared to be energy moving about the players in the huddle.
>
> Then I heard a voice say, "This will be the golden season. I will remove the oppressive cloud that has been upon this team and I will fulfill promises that I have made to Bill McCartney. My power will move upon the players and My spirit will touch many of them. This will be their golden season." I looked up to see where the voice came from and I saw spacious, clear blue skies with just enough shade clouds to block out the heat of the sun. The voice spoke again, "I will bring this team under clear skies of wisdom, understanding, and knowledge, and I will shade them from the heat of public scrutiny and criticism."[33]

Both McCartney and Ryle took the dream seriously (the date is even listed in the chronology of events surrounding McCartney's tenure at Colorado that introduces the book). The interpretation of dreams has a long history in both secular and Christian culture. In secular culture, dreams are taken seriously, but as a symptom of psychological chemistry – a symptom of one's own psyche and/or spirit – but not as a direct communication from God. Christian tradition has not looked favorably on modern day prophets, thus the skepticism concerning the Vineyard.

McCartney has had his own vision, though not as dramatic as Ryle's golden season dream. McCartney describes the conceptualization of Promise Keepers in March 1990 as a vision and dream he shared with Dave Wardell.[34] As the two were driving to a meeting for the Fellowship of Christian Athletes, they exchanged answers to the question "If money were not an issue, and you could do anything you wanted with your life, what would you do?"[35]

McCartney describes the conversation and his feelings in the following manner:

> "More than anything," I told him, "God has put it in my heart to witness a tremendous outpouring of His Spirit upon men. I envision men coming together in huge numbers in the name of Jesus, worshiping and celebrating their faith together. I long to see men openly proclaiming their love for Christ and their commitment to their families." The vision I shared with him is one that I had been feeling in my heart for some time.[36]

McCartney concludes this discussion by stating how he and Wardell "discussed our dreams further and agreed to pray about our desires," and how they shared their "vision" with a handful of friends.[37]

The first time I read McCartney's autobiography I knew nothing of Ryle and the Vineyard. I took the use of words such as 'dream' and 'vision' to mean just that, one's dreams and ideas about how the future might unfold. But read in the context of Vineyard, the reliance on dreams and visions takes on another meaning, perhaps distancing PK leadership from generally accepted Christian theology.

Besides the influence of the Vineyard and pastor Ryle, the Promise Keepers are supported and influenced by a diverse group of evangelical men. The Promise Keepers have received support from a wide range of Christian evangelical groups, including the most prominent evangelical in America, Billy Graham. As stated above, there are both traditional and new evangelicals involved in the Promise Keepers organization. This section places individual Promise Keepers into three categories: traditional, new, and not easily categorized.

*Traditional Evangelicals*

The majority of Promise Keepers can be categorized as traditional evangelicals, although often they are more charismatic than other evangelicals. One example of a PK traditional evangelical is Dr. Ed Cole, founder and president of the Christian Men's Network. Cole, a PK conference speaker and author of *Maximize Manhood*, has devoted almost thirty years to "organizing Christian men and holding separate retreats for them."[38] *Maximized Manhood* has been described as the "forerunner of current Promise Keepers ideology."[39] Cole has characterized the women in the feminist movement as "bitter and empty" because "any movement that ignores God is headed for trouble."[40]

Another traditional evangelical, but with earnest charismatic beliefs, is Dr. Jack Hayford. Hayford is a PK conference speaker and the Senior pastor of Church on the Way, Van Nuys, California. Hayford serves on the board of directors for National Religious Broadcasters (NRB) and World Impact, a church planting ministry for America's inner cities. NRB is an association of nearly 1,000 evangelical Christian radio and television stations and program producers. NRB's Homepage states that the association "exists to represent the Christian broadcasters' right to communicate the Gospel of Jesus Christ to a lost and dying world." The 1998 NRB Convention, billed as the "Largest Gathering of Christian Communication Professionals," was headlined by Elizabeth Dole and William Bennett.

Hayford also operates KTLW, a radio station in Los Angeles and part of the Living Way radio network. The broadcast directory lists typical evangelical Christian radio programming, such as James Dobson's *Focus on the Family*, Joseph Stowell's *Proclaim*, Bob Phillips' *Bible Commentary*, and Chuck Swindoll's *Insight for Living*.

Hayford is also the senior editorial advisor for Strang Communication's *Ministries Today* magazine. In a 1996 interview titled "The State of the Union" in *Charisma* magazine, another Strang Communication product, Hayford, along with nine other Christian leaders, including Promise Keepers Bill Bright and Raleigh Washington, was asked "How should Christians be praying at this crucial hour, particularly as we face this election?" Hayford responded with the following:

> I don't think we are called to pray against a person or a party but against evil. If we fast and pray, just as in Esther's time, the power of evil will be broken and "the gallows of Haman" set in place--while God roots out whatever may be the true source of our national dilemma.[41]

Bright and Washington responded with similar sentiments.

Other notable traditional evangelical board members[42] and speakers include the following:

- ❑ Ronald Blue is the founder of a financial planning firm in Atlanta, Georgia. He also serves on the board of directors for Chuck Swindoll's *Insight for Living*, Gary Bauer's *Family Research Council* (a new evangelical organization and part of Dobson's *Focus on the Family* from 1988-1992), and Bill Bright's *Campus Crusade for Christ International.*
- ❑ Dr. Jesse Miranda is a PK conference speaker and an associate dean of Urban and Multi-Cultural Affairs, Haggard School of Theology, Azusa Pacific University, Azusa, California. He is also the president and founding member of Alianza de Ministerios Evanglelicos Nacionales (AMEN – Alliance of National Evangelical Ministries).
- ❑ Dr. A.R. Bernard is the Senior Pastor, Christian Life Center, Brooklyn, NY, and a member of the board of directors for the Cole's Christian Men's Network.
- ❑ Dr. David Bryant is the founder and president of Concerts of Prayer International, Wheaton, IL. He is also chairman of the National Prayer Committee and former pastor for InterVarsity Christian Fellowship/USA.
- ❑ Dr. Tony Evans is the senior pastor at Oak Cliff Bible Fellowship in Dallas, TX. He is also founder and president of The Urban Alternative.
- ❑ Rev. Franklin Graham is president of Samaritan's Purse, a nonprofit Christian relief and evangelism organization "that specializes in meeting the needs of victims of war, poverty, natural disasters, and disease."[43] He is the son of evangelist Billy Graham and serves on the Billy Graham Evangelistic Association board of directors which manages Graham's extensive ministry.
- ❑ Pastor Bill Hybels is the senior pastor of the Willow Creek megachurch in South Barrington, IL, which shares Vineyard Ministries commitment to contemporary worship. Hybels is coauthor of *Becoming a Contagious Christian.*
- ❑ Dr. Crawford Loritts, Jr., is the national director of Legacy Ministries in Union City, GA, and the director of the 1997 National Congress on the Urban Family.
- ❑ Keith Phillips is president of World Impact, Inc., in Los Angeles, and a member of Urban Ministries Resources Editorial Advisory Board of Zondervan Publishing House, an evangelical press. Phillips is also a board member of the Christian Community Development Association and chairman of the Los Angeles Mayor's Prayer Breakfast.

❑ Gary Smalley is president of Today's Family in Branson, MO, and a popular speaker on family relationships. He is the host of the television infomercial "Hidden Keys to Loving Relationships."

❑ Dr. Joseph M. Stowell is president of the Moody Bible Institute in Chicago.

❑ Dr. Bruce Wilkinson is founder and president of Walk Thru the Bible Ministries, headquartered in Atlanta, GA and branch offices in 14 countries. Walk Thru the Bible is an international publishing and training organization with a teaching faculty of "120 in North America and 2,000 instructors around the world."[44] Wilkinson is also chairman of The CoMission, an international movement sending 12,000 Christians to the former Soviet Union for a year of ministry service.[45]

Ken Abraham's book *Who Are the Promise Keepers?* provides an example of traditional evangelical boosterism. The book cover makes the claim that the book will provide an indepth commentary on the organization from a well-known writer who "acts as the eyes and ears of an inquisitive person who hears about Promise Keepers and wonders what it is all about." Abraham's conclusion regarding the question "Who are the Promise Keepers?" is ". . . like it or not – they are who they say they are."[46] For Abraham, this means they are men who want to build a deeper relationship with Jesus, shed their selfish desires and work to transform society, and be better husbands, fathers, and brothers.[47]

There may be nothing inaccurate about Abraham's perspective concerning the Promise Keepers. He offers a sympathetic view of Promise Keepers, but one could question the "eyes and ears of this inquisitive person" when one learns that Abraham is less than the objective author he presents himself to be. Abraham has a direct affiliation with Promise Keepers as an author in one of their earlier projects. Five years before his book *Who Are the Promise Keepers?* was published, Abraham contributed three articles to Bill McCartney's *What Makes a Man?* In the articles, Abraham echoes common Promise Keepers themes. He discusses the futility of "trying to be 'good' under" one's own power, the struggles of a Christian to maintain his values when those values are challenged by others, particularly friends, and the societal problems caused by adultery and how a man can avoid temptation and maintain accountability on business trips.[48]

This earlier association with Promise Keepers is never discussed in *Who Are the Promise Keepers?* Perhaps Abraham's conclusion that the Promise Keepers are simply who they say they are would be more appropriately stated as "We Promise Keepers are who we say we are."

*New Evangelicals*

As stated above, traditional evangelicals are modeled after the work of Billy Graham and new evangelicals model the political activism of the Pat Robertson's ministry. An example of a new evangelical is Charles W. Colson, founder and chairman of the board of Prison Fellowship Ministries. Colson is a PK conference speaker and contributor to *Go the Distance*. He is the host of the daily radio commentary "Breakpoint," which attempts to foster a political discussion of morality and individual responsibility. In *Go the Distance*, Colson's section is called "A Man and His Integrity." Colson, special counsel to President Nixon who was convicted for his involvement in Watergate, discusses the tyranny of one's pride, the importance of duty, his acceptance of Jesus Christ, and one's rationalization of sin. Colson also discusses how Christians can change their society, through both their actions and lack thereof. Colson uses himself as an example of one who did not place matters in God's hands, reminding the reader of his criminal involvement in Watergate. He concludes by calling men to be men of integrity, describing one's integrity as not a "parochial matter" but one "of life-and-death importance to this nation."[49]

Another book by Colson, *A Dance With Deception: Revealing the Truth Behind the Headline*, is a collection of Breakpoint commentaries. In the book, Colson comments on such social issues as domestic partnership laws, diversity training, and gays in the military. When discussing date rape, Colson states: "The 1960s sowed the slogans of free sex," free of its moral foundations, and "today we are reaping a harvest of forced sex."[50] Thus, according to Colson, date rape is the logical outcome of man's Machiavellian nature; men, unhindered by moral concerns, will take what they want when they want it.

A new evangelical booster who provided early financial support through a donation to Promise Keepers as they were beginning their ministry is James Dobson, founder of Focus on the Family.[51] Focus on the Family also provides broadcast support and publishes many of the Promise Keepers study guides and books, including *The Power of a Promise Kept* and *Go The Distance*. They also maintain a presence at PK stadium conferences with a booth in the ministry section, where they provide pamphlets and sell books and videos. Dobson has also contributed an article to McCartney's *What Makes a Man?* where he discusses "A Man and His Work."

Pat Robertson's 700 Club has also provided promotional segments for Promise Keepers events and conferences. The August 1997 PK News ran the following headline: "Promise Keepers, 700 Club Join Forces for Stand in the Gap."[52] According to Andy Freeman, executive producer of the 700 Club, Robertson's organization "wants to stand in unity with Promise Keepers to promote Stand in the Gap."[53] In doing so, the organization produced six segments promoting various aspects of the assembly, including Bill McCartney's discussion of the goals for the assembly on September 30, immediately prior to the gathering.

Another new evangelical involved with Promise Keepers is Dr. Bill Bright, author of *The Coming Revival: America's Call To Fast, Pray and "Seek God's Face"* and *Promises: Daily Devotion for Supernatural Living*. Bright is the founder and President of Campus Crusade for Christ International and a PK conference speaker. His Campus Crusade for Christ is a worldwide interdenominational ministry with 13,000 fulltime staff and over 100,000 trained volunteers. Volunteers for Campus Crusade for Christ serve in prisons, the military, athletic organizations, and college campuses, among others. Bright is also a contributing author to *Seven Promises of a Promise Keeper*, where he discusses the power of Christian love.

Bill Bright's Campus Crusade for Christ International is also a cosponsor (with Mission America) of the annual *Fasting and Prayer* conference. The 1997 conference was convened in Dallas on November 12-14, with PK Wellington Boone, Shirley Dobson, Pat Robertson, and PK Tony Evans. In 1996 both PK President Randy Phillips and Bill McCartney were speakers. Promise Keepers Bill McCartney, Bill Bright, Jesse Miranda, Franklin Graham, and David Bryant, along with Pat Robertson, form six of the nine members of the Executive Committee for *Fasting and Prayer 1997.*[54] Using the same evangelical terminology as the PK Washington, D.C. sacred assembly[55], notwithstanding the involvement of Pat Robertson, this annual conference focuses on spiritual renewal rather than political activism.

There are at least two examples of Bill Bright's direct involvement in political activity. In 1996, along with other Promise Keepers John Perkins, Chuck Colson, and Charles Swindol, and 16 other Christian leaders, including James Dobson and Paul Cedar, he signed a letter addressed to the Republican party leadership. In the letter, the signers "expressed concern about the campaign by some prominent Republicans to delete or modify the prolife plank in the party's platform."[56] The letter urged the Republican leadership to continue their support of a constitutional amendment banning abortion.

The other example of Bright's activism is his involvement with the Coalition on Revival (COR), recently renamed The Alliance for Revival & Reformation. In 1988, Bright was the "Plenary Speaker at COR's ratification of the 42 Articles."[57] COR is a restorationist evangelical organization of Christian leaders. On July 4, 1986, it declared its foundational theology in the organization's *Declaration and Convenant* (DC). COR advocates a restoration of biblical principles in public life, "The Christian Church must be the Salt and Light to the World."[58] Included in the *Declaration and Covenant* are a list of "Social Evils to Oppose" and the affirmation that "all Bible-believing Christians must take a nonneutral stance in opposing, praying against, and speaking against social moral evils."[59] The list includes common Christian moral issues such as the unjust treatment of the poor and disadvantaged, abortion on demand, pornography, and euthanasia, but it also includes several political and economic positions that place the group firmly with the Christian Right. Some examples include:

1. State usurpation of parental rights and God given liberties.

2. Statist-collectivist theft from citizens through devaluation of their money and redistribution of their wealth.

3. Atheism, moral relativism, and evolutionism taught as a monopoly viewpoint in public schools.

4. Communism/Marxism, fascism, Nazism and the one world government of the New Age Movement.

The document, affirmed in 1986 and listed on the Alliance's Homepage in 1997 (repent.org), along with *The Chicago Statement on Biblical Inerrancy*, outline the new evangelical, ecumenical, and restorationist (dominionism) principles of the organization. Formed and directed by an executive committee of four (Jay Grimstead, Pierre Bynum, Pat Mahoney, and Harry Valentine) and a 37-member steering committee, COR is a counter to the theology of dispensationalism. Dispensationalism emphasizes "the futility of trying to change the world in the current age, maintaining that Christ has the authority to reign but has chosen not to exercise it until he returns."[60] COR argues otherwise, that "Christ is now reigning, and his followers with him,"[61] and that the "Church must stand to fulfill the Great Commission."[62] The distinction fundamentally affects how one views activism. On the one hand, dispensationalists believe Christ could reign if he wanted to, but he has chosen not to. COR believes he is reigning, and all (real) Christians must help him reign. With Christ on their side, COR advocates an evangelical activism that "proposes Christian takeovers in virtually all aspects of human endeavor: education, the arts, politics, and even the military".[63]

There are also many similarities between the Promise Keepers movement and COR, at least concerning language and intentions. In 1996, the Alliance held a "National Solemn Assembly" of church leaders in Washington, D.C., to "repent, to seek God, and to pray for our beloved nation" (this is also when the group renamed itself The Alliance for Revival & Reformation). In 1997, Promise Keepers held A Sacred Assembly of Men with the purpose of calling men to "repent before Almighty, Holy God" and to "seek His face and pray so that He might pour out His Holy Spirit to heal our land."[64] Both groups emphasize 2 Chronicles 7:14[65] as a call to pray for the nation. Both groups plan on "going global" after the year 2000 with their ministries. Also, The Alliance for Revival & Reformation listed its only national Steering Committee Meeting for October 2, 1997, arranged as an opportunity "to piggyback Promise Keepers' Stand in the Gap Gathering in Washington, D.C."[66]

It has also been reported that several Promise Keepers have been associated with COR. Promise Keeper Bishop Wellington Boone is founder and president of Wellington Boone Ministries, Atlanta, GA, and also a board member for March for Jesus.[67] He is the author of *Breaking Through: Taking the Kingdom into the Culture by Out-Serving Others*. Boone, a prominent speaker at PK conferences, offers a message of "genuine humility" to be used in serving others. His ministry encourages men and women to reach beyond race barriers to form multiracial prayer groups.

But Boone's involvement with COR seems to be extensive. Joe Conason, Alfred Ross, and Lee Cokorinos reported in *The Nation* that Boone was a member of COR's executive committee, editor and columnist for its theoretical journal *Crosswinds*, and the head of COR's black mobilization seminar project.[68]

Conason et al., also report involvement of other Promise Keepers with COR, including, Joseph Garlington, E.V. Hill, and John Perkins. Garlington is a PK speaker and the Senior Pastor at Covenant Church of Pittsburgh, a nondenominational, multiracial ministry. E.V. Hill serves as vice president of the National Baptist Convention, USA, board member for Billy Graham Evangelistic Association, and at the National Institute on Biblical Inerrancy.[69] Dr. John Perkins, founder and president of the John Perkins Foundation for biblical and economic justice, is the publisher of the *Urban Family Magazine*.

All four men are black, causing concerns among some commentators that the Christian Right is recruiting within the black congregations.[70] Conason et al., report that all the men are part of COR's steering committee. Recent correspondence with COR, under the new name of The Alliance for Revival & Reformation, did not list any of the men as serving on either its executive or steering committees. Their relationships, in the capacity reported by Conason et al., has been discontinued, at least publicly.

With their previous official association with COR, these four Promise Keepers appear to be involved in what I have been referring to as new evangelicalism. The similarities between COR and Promise Keepers semantics and assembly is important to note, but it is less than clear how this "relationship" would affect PK ministry, particularly in its less than COR like demands, or how it might affect the men involved in Promise Keepers at a local level.

That leaves Bill McCartney himself. McCartney has a long history of political involvement, including speaking engagements at Operation Rescue events and his advisory position on the board of Colorado for Family Values, which sponsored the Colorado's Amendment 2, which forbade government from enacting legislation that would give homosexuals protected status or the right to claim discrimination. He has also appeared several times on the 700 Club with Pat Robertson and serves on the board of *Fasting and Prayer* with Robertson.

In a recent article in *Policy Review*, published by The Heritage Foundation, McCartney states that "social problems are moral problems, which ultimately have a spiritual cause."[71] These are the same sentiments found in COR's *Declaration and Covenant*, and seem to lead to the form of activism recommended by other new evangelicals.

As we have seen, the Promise Keepers board members and the men who speak at conferences come from diverse organizations and denominations. What they share in common is an evangelical and ecumenical spirit. They are the leaders of large congregations and small shelters. They are the publishers and instructors of Christian self-help programs. Some of them are leading the evangelical movement in postcommunist countries, while others are involved in outreach programs in urban America. The defining difference between them is how they perceive the role of evangelical activism; is the Great Commission an individual act or a political responsibility? As stated above, traditional evangelicals model Billy Graham's work of personal conversion and mass evangelism. It is the influence of new evangelicals at the leadership levels, the Oval Office model, that give the Promise Keepers the look of a crypto-Christian Right group. But as I argued in the first chapter, the effect of any crypto-Christian Right ideology on the men involved at the local level appears to be negligible. The men I interviewed and encountered were almost singularly concerned with individual salvation and not national salvation.

*Opposition – Liberal and Christian*

Not surprisingly, the Promise Keepers generate a good deal of criticism. A movement that consists of mostly white men congregating in football stadiums, preaching a message of biblical reconciliation, and encouraging each other to form a men's small group, is bound to have many critics. The Promise Keepers receive criticism from liberals, radical feminists, moderate Christians, and even other evangelicals. The Promise Keepers have been described as homophobic,[72] advocates of male supremacy,[73] men who do not support women's equality,[74] radical ecumenicist,[75] unduly influenced by psychobabble Christianity,[76] heretics who claim God speaks directly to them in dreams,[77] and Promise Weepers, symptomatic of Clinton's America.[78]

Until recently, liberal criticism was sporadic and unorganized. It consisted of articles in popular magazines, press releases, and, too often, misinformation and hyperbole. The criticisms primarily centered on Promise Keepers positions regarding women and homosexuality.

The Promise Keepers Sacred Assembly has given liberal critics new vigor in their opposition to the movement. The National Gay and Lesbian Task Force's (NGLTF) executive director, Kerry Lobel, issued a statement concerning the "hidden agenda of the Promise Keepers movement" at a press conference organized by the National Organization for Women. According to NGLTF, the Promise Keepers "pledge to strengthen families scapegoats woman and gay people, blaming them for the collapse of family and community."[79] The NGLTF also criticized the Promise Keepers commitment to racial reconciliation, stating that "Their pledge of racial reconciliation rings hollow without a commitment to overcoming institutional racism."[80] NGLTF's conclusion is that the Promise Keepers perpetuate "racial and gender oppression and homophobia."[81]

Emotions, which are fundamental to the Promise Keepers experience, are a point of contention in Christian theology. If one feels the Lord and the Holy Spirit, one lays claim to a holy experience through the bodily vessel. This is an interpretation based on bodily emotions. But if one feels lust for another person this bodily emotion is considered a sin. So, one emotional experience is deemed holy, the other sinful, but both interpretations rely on the body as the medium of interpellation.

The Promise Keepers, as well as other evangelical organizations, have been criticized for their reliance on emotions and what they feel in their heart. This criticism has Scriptural foundations. The issue is addressed in David Hagopian and Douglas Wilson's *Beyond Promises: A Biblical Challenge to Promise Keepers*. Hagopian and Wilson refer to Jeremiah 17:9, which states "The heart is deceitful above all things and beyond cure. Who can understand it?" Their criticism is that too often Promise Keepers turn to what is in one's heart rather than what is God's will. In other words, if the heart and emotions are deceitful and beyond cure, how then can one ever trust one's emotions; how can one know an emotional state indicates God's will? Hagopian and Wilson conclude that "Because the human heart is not naturally good, it cannot be where we (Christians) turn to find the biblical pattern for anything, let alone worship."[82]

Another criticism from Christians concerns the interpretation of dreams and visions by Promise Keepers leadership. This was discussed above when referring to the spawning of Promise Keepers from the Vineyard movement, but Bill McCartney has also felt the call of the Holy Spirit. Bill McCartney has claimed that at the first Promise Keepers conference in 1991, after noticing the crowd was mainly white men, "the Spirit of God clearly said to my spirit, 'You can fill that stadium, but if men of other races aren't there, I won't be there, either.'"[83] This message from God has been criticized by Christian commentators, not because they disagree with the message of racial reconciliation, but because McCartney seems to counter Scripture. Hagopian and Douglas point out that in Matthew 18:20, Jesus is quoted as saying "For where two or three come together in my name, there am I with them."[84] By relying on Scripture to support their critique of McCartney's vision, Hagopian and Douglas expose a historical fissure within Christian theology regarding the interpretation of the Bible as it relates to a developing social movement. It also highlights the fact that the most accurate opposition to Promise Keepers will use the same critical techniques used by PK – the word of God.

## Concluding Thought

The main criticism of PK will continue to come from conservative and liberal Christians because they are accepted as believers and their critiques are biblically based. Feminists will have little impact on the movement other than as the enemy, Promise Keepers' Nebraska. Feminists are not listened to because they are seen as part of the problem rather than the solution.

Promise Keepers is, for the most part, a traditional evangelical movement at the local level and a mix of traditional and new at the leadership level. But that does not explain the essential nature of Promise Keepers, which is of a social, rather than personal or political, quality. Even though PK has elements of both new and traditional evangelicalism, it offers another form of evangelicalism, a form I refer to as social evangelicalism. Social evangelicalism is based on social relationships rather than personal salvation (Lincoln Bedroom model) or political activism (Oval Office model). It is an evangelical ministry based on the reconciliation of a man to his relationship with God, his wife, children, family, friends, and coworkers.

As is often the case with social movements, the leadership does not always reflect the mass. How Promise Keepers develops in the future will depend on how much influence the new evangelicals have in developing and shaping Promise Keepers ministry. The counsel in an editorial in *Christianity Today* summarizes the dilemma. It argues that the challenge confronting Promise Keepers is "how to be socially and morally engaged in society without succumbing to a narrow political agenda."[85] This dilemma appears to be resolved in social evangelicalism. As long as the traditional evangelicals are influencing Promise Keepers and PK maintains its focus on reconciliation and relationship building, the movement can socially and morally engage society without succumbing to a political agenda, the Lincoln Bedroom model of evangelicalism. When one begins discussing new evangelicals, the Oval Office model of influence, one enters a rather narrow political agenda.

## Notes

1. Robert Booth Fowler, and Allen D. Hertzke, *Religion and Politics in America: Faith, Culture, and Strategic Choices* (Boulder, CO: Westview Press, 1995), 38.

2. Robert Zweir, *Born-Again Politics: The New Christian Right in America* (Downers Grove, IL: InterVarsity Press, 1982), 37-45. See also Clyde Wilcox, *God's Warriors: The Christian Right in Twentieth-Century America* (Baltimore, MD: The Johns Hopkins University Press, 1992), 213-216; Kenneth D. Wald, *Religion and Politics in the United States*, 3rd ed. (Washington, DC: Congressional Quarterly Press, 1996), 217-266.

3. David W. Bebbington, "Evangelicalism in Its Settings: The British and American Movements Since 1940," in *Evangelicalism: Comparative Studies of Popular Protestantism in North America, British Isles, and Beyond, 1700-1990*, ed. Mark A. Noll, David W. Bebbington, and George A. Rawlyk (Oxford: Oxford University Press, 1994), 27. See also Gabriel Fackre, *Ecumenical Faith in Evangelical Perspective* (Grand Rapids, MI: William B. Eerdmans Publishing, 1993), 22-23; Fowler and Hertzke, *Religion and Politics in America*, 36-37.

4. Fackre, *Ecumenical Faith in Evangelical Perspective,* 22.

5. See Fowler and Hertzke, *Religion and Politics in America,* 36-39.

6. Frederick Clarkson, "Righteous Brothers," *In These Times* (August 5, 1996), 16. See also Michael S. Kimmel, "Promise Keepers: Patriarchy's Second Coming as Masculine Renewal," *TIKKUN* 12, no. 2 (February 1996), 49-50; Sterling Research Associates, *Promise Keepers: The Third Wave of the American Religious Right* (New York: Sterling Research Associates, 1996), 3; R. Lorraine Bernotsky, and Joan M. Bernotsky, "Promise Keepers: Politics and Religion in a Contemporary Men's Movement," Paper Presented at the *American Political Science Association* (August

1997), 14; John M. Swomley, "Storm Troopers in the Culture War," *The Humanist* (September/October 1997), 8-13.

7. Bill McCartney, with Dave Diles, *From Ashes to Glory* (Nashville: Thomas Nelson Publishers, 1995), 219. (Original work published in 1990.) See also Bill McCartney, with David Halbrook, *Sold Out* (Nashville: Word Publishing, 1997), 109-115.

8. Bill McCartney, "Seeking God's Favor," in *Seven Promises of a Promise Keeper*, ed. Al Janssen (Colorado Springs: Focus on the Family Publishing, 1994), 207.

9. Bill McCartney, "It's Time for Men to Take a Stand," in *What Makes a Man?* ed. Stephen Griffith (Colorado Springs: NavPress Publishing Group, 1992), 11.

10. McCartney, *From Ashes to Glory*, 222.

11. Ibid., 222.

12. Bill McCartney, *Stand In The Gap: The Prayer Journal* (Dallas: Word Publishing, 1997), 15-16.

13. McCartney, *From Ashes to Glory*, 246.

14. Ibid., 185. The full passage discusses adversity and coaching: "In my heart, I believe strong men lead weak men. All down through history, strong men have been able to rally and incite and motivate and challenge other men to perform great deeds, to accomplish even what they feel they cannot. At that point in my career, I was being anything but strong. It was time to quit moaning and saying, "Why me, God?" and get on with the business at hand."

15. Promise Keepers Homepage, promisekeepers.org (October 1997).

16. Promise Keepers Key Man Brochure (1996).

17. Promise Keepers Key Man Training Pamphlet (1995), 2.

18. Ibid., 2-6.

19. Promise Keepers Ambassador Pamphlet (1996).

20. Promise Keepers Ambassador Training Level One (1996), 2.

21. Promise Keepers Homepage, promisekeepers.org (October 1997).

22. Promise Keepers Statement of Faith.

23. For a similar discussion see Kenneth Clatterbaugh, *Contemporary Perspectives on Masculinity: Men, Women, and Politics in Modern Society,* 2nd ed. (Boulder, CO: Westview Press, 1997), 176.

24. McCartney, *From Ashes to Glory*, 291. At a Key Man and Ambassador training session I attended, a list "of individuals to whom we may need to be reconciled" was distributed. The list included "wife, son, daughter, mother, father, brother, sister, neighbor, pastor, former friend, white person, Black person, Hispanic person, Native American person, Asian person, difficult person."

25. Friedrich Nietzsche, *Beyond Good and Evil*, trans. R.J. Hollingdale (New York: Penguin Books, 1990), 75-77. (Original work published 1886.)

26. Fackre, *Ecumenical Faith in Evangelical Perspective*, 23.

27. Scott Raab, "Triumph of His Will," *GQ* (January 1996), 129.

28. See Debra Bouey, "James Ryle's Vineyard Theology," *The Christian Conscience* (Reprint, February 1996), 1-2; Lynn Leslie, and Sarah Leslie, "The New Gnostics: Resurrecting Pagan Rites – Part 3," *The Christian Conscience* (Reprint, February 1996), 2; Carl Widrig, Jr., "Is God Saying What James Ryle is Saying?" *The Christian Conscience* (Reprint, May 1996), 1-6; Russ Bellant, "Mania in the Stadia: The Origins and Goals of Promise Keepers," *Front Lines Research* (May 1995), 7-9.

29. Vineyard Christian Fellowship Boulder Valley Homepage (July 1997). The Homepage is www.oneimage.com/~wfields/vine/.

30. James Ryle, *Hippo in the Garden: A Non Religious Approach to having a Conversation with God* (Orlando, FL: Creation House, 1993), 48.

31. McCartney, *From Ashes to Glory*, 112.

32. Ibid., xviii; 49; 269.

33. Ibid., 49-50.

34. Ibid., 286.

35. Ibid., 285.

36. Ibid., 286.

37. Ibid., 286.

38. Clatterbaugh, *Contemporary Perspectives on Masculinity*, 178.

39. Ibid., 178.

40. Jim Nelson Black, "The Heart of the New Man," *New Man* (November-December 1994), 66.

41. Richard Ciznik, "The State of the Union," *Charisma* (Orlando, FL: Strang Communications, 1996), 22. Bright and Washington responded with similar sentiments.

42. The following is a complete list of the PK board of directors as of October, 1997; Dick Blair, Ron Blue, Huron Claus, Dr. Jack Hayford, Dr. Howard Hendricks, E. Peb Jackson, Bill McCartney, Dr. Jesse Miranda, Pastor George Morrison, Dr. Gary J. Oliver, Sid Overton, Harry W. (Hank) Peters, Bishop Phillip H. Porter, David Roadcup, Pastor James Ryle, Alonzo E. Short, Jr., and Michael Timmis. The President of PK is Randy Phillips.

43. Samaritan's Purse Homepage, samaritan.org/spintro.htm (1997).

44. Walk Thru the Bible Homepage, walkthru.org (1997).

45. Promise Keepers Homepage, promisekeepers.org (September 1997).

46. Ken Abraham, *Who Are the Promise Keepers?: Understanding the Christian Men's Movement* (New York: Doubleday, 1997), 202.

47. Ibid., 202.

48. See Ken Abraham, "God Loves Losers, Too!" "Acceptance at What Price?" "Traveler's Advisory," in *What Makes A Man?*, ed. Stephen Griffith (Colorado Springs: NavPress, 1992), 56-57, 128-129, 163-165.

49. Charles W. Colson, "A Man and His Integrity," in *Go the Distance*, ed. John Trent (Colorado Springs: Focus on the Family Publishing, 1996), 112.

50. Charles W. Colson, with Nancy R. Pearcey, *A Dance With Deception: Revealing the Truth Behind the Headline* (Dallas: Word Publishing, 1993), 167.

51. Raab, "Triumph of His Will," 128.

52. Promise Keepers Homepage, promisekeepers.org (September 1997).

53. Ibid.

54. A complete list includes McCartney, Robertson, Thomas E. Trask of the General Council of the Assemblies of God, PK Jesse Miranda, Paul Cedar of Mission America, PK Franklin Graham, Don Argue, president of the National Association of Evangelicals, PK David Bryant, and Kay Arthur, president of Precept ministries.

55. Fasting and Prayer 97 Homepage, ccci.org/fasting-prayer/home.html (September 1997); "If my people, who are called by my name, will humble themselves and pray and seek my face and turn from their wicked ways, then will I hear from heaven and will forgive their sin and will heal their land" (2 Chronicles 7:14, NIV); and also "Stand in the gap! Be an intercessory vessel for God at this critical time. We believe it is a matter of

life and death for our nation. Also, please tell others and ask them to join you at this historic Fasting & Prayer '97."

56. Tom Strode, "3 SBC Pastors Join Call for GOP to stay Pro-Life," *Baptist Press News* (March 12, 1996), 3.

57. Ed Tarkowski, "Part Two: Foundations For Apostasy: 1986-1996," manuscript (1996), 1.

58. *Declaration and Covenant* (1986), 8. From the manifesto: "The world will not know how to live or which direction to go without the Church's biblical influence on its theories, laws, actions, and institutions. To be salt and light, the Church cannot exist in a Christian "ghetto" or have a dichotomous view that falsely divides life into spiritual versus the physical-historical-measurable" (8).

59. Ibid., 8.

60. Randy Frame, "Is Christ or Satan Ruler of This World?" *Christianity Today* (March 5, 1990), 42.

61. Ibid., 42.

62. Tarkowski, "Part Two: Foundations For Apostasy," 1.

63. Randy Frame, "Plan Calls for Doing Away with Public Schools, IRS," *Christianity Today* (November 19, 1990), 57.

64. Promise Keepers *Stand in the Gap* Brochure (1997).

65. 2 Chronicles 7:14 "If my people, which are called by my name, shall humble themselves, and pray, and seek my face, and turn from their wicked ways; then will I hear from heaven, and will forgive their sin, and will heal their land."

66. The Alliance for Revival & Reformation Homepage, www.repent.org (October 1997).

67. March for Jesus is an international nondenominational Christian prayer and demonstration group.

68. Joe Conason, Alfred Ross, and Lee Cokorinos, "The Promise Keepers are Coming: The Third Wave of the Religious Right," *The Nation* (October 7, 1996), 14. See also Conrad F. Goeringer, "Godly Men with a Dominionist Agenda," *American Atheist* (Reprint, Spring 1997), 2-16.

69. Promise Keepers Homepage, promisekeepers.org (September 1997).

70. Michael S. Kimmel, "Promise Keepers: Patriarchy's Second Coming as Masculine Renewal," *TIKKUN* 12, no. 2 (February 1996), 49; Frederick Clarkson, "Righteous Brothers," *In These Times* (August 5, 1996), 16.

71. Bill McCartney, "Promise Makers," *Policy Review* (Reprint, September-October 1997), 1.

72. Kerry Lobel, National Gay and Lesbian Task Force Press Statement: Promise Keepers (June 13, 1997), 1.

73. Kimmel, "Promise Keepers," 50.

74. Patricia Ireland, "A Look At . . . Promise Keepers: Beware of 'Feel-Good Male Supremacy,'" *Washington Post* (September 7, 1997), C03.

75. Phil Arms, *Promise Keepers: Another Trojan Horse* (Houston, TX: Shiloh Publishers, 1997), 243-245.

76. David Hagopian, and Douglas Wilson, *Beyond Promises: A Biblical Challenge to Promise Keepers* (Moscow, ID: Canon Press, 1996), 75-92.

77. Carl Widrig, Jr. "Is God Saying What James Ryle is Saying?" *The Christian Conscience* (Reprint, May 1996), 2.

78. Hanna Rogin, "Promise Weepers," *The New Republic* (October 27, 1997), 11-12.

79. The National Gay and Lesbian Task Force's Statement (1997), 1.

80. Ibid., 2.

81. Ibid., 2. See also Kimmel, "Promise Keepers," 49-50.

82. Hagopian and Wilson, *Beyond Promises*, 149.

83. McCartney, "Seeking God's Favor," 160.

84. Hagopian and Wilson, *Beyond Promises*, 156-158.

85. Howard A. Snyder, "Will Promise Keepers Keep Their Promises?" *Christianity Today* (November 14, 1994), 20-21.

## Chapter Three

---

# The Promise Keepers as Social Capitalists

> Our society is walking down a deadly path of moral relativism. All values are at best negotiable and at worst nonexistent. Every day we're influenced by the philosophy and values of those around us. And as Christian men, it's possible to become numb to that relativistic influence without even noticing it.
>
> Gregg Lewis, *The Power of a Promise Kept*

The locution "moral relativism" is a stylish label for discussing the tribulations of modern civil society. The familiar explanation is that civil society has been deconstructed to the point that it is no longer clear what it values, how it functions, or how its members are supposed to contribute to it. Members are often described as being detached, passionless, and indifferent to traditional community standards. They are characterized as lost in a "culture of disbelief" or searching for a culture to believe in.

The epigraph to this essay, with only minor alterations, could be taken from any number of popular articles and books on the subject of civil society and its moral underpinnings. So the story goes, historically, civil society has always already been an effort to discriminate between good and evil, its power being grounded in the ability to sanction and/or displace value judgments. Through both repressive and ideological forces, (most) members of a civil society were trained to easily and consistently distinguish good from evil. This is the nostalgic, and usually romantic, depiction of civil society. It is nostalgic (and popular) because it conjures up a less confusing time when value judgments were made with firmness and without hesitation. It is also romantic because it easily forgets that every value judgment of "good" is also simultaneously a statement of exclusion, demarcating the accepted from the refused and the sacred from the profane.

As contemporary civil society hurtles onward, it does so without the confidence and hubris of previous societies. Its displaced and fragmented elements, continuing to articulate and elicit expressions of value, are compelled to have and declare some value, *any* value. To gain understanding of the *bricolage* of value declarations called civil society, it is not apparent where one should begin. Some sociopolitical theorists have started with an investigation of the dominant institutions and detailed their influence in creating and perpetuating the social individual. Others have begun by privileging the individual and his or her ability to determine and declare the values that a society and its institutions should promote and sustain. But perhaps it is unimportant where one begins in attempting to understand civil society. For those who feel lost in their own community, who no longer feel confident in deploying their value judgments, who feel they are walking down the deadly path of moral relativism, it is less important where one begins as long as one begins somewhere.

If civil society is a *bricolage* of value judgments, it is also the exchange of commitments and promises between individuals, groups, and institutions. Simply put, civil society is a relationship that presupposes shared values and calculable individuals. Why must individuals be "calculable"? Because civil society demands not only that members share many of the same values, but also that there is a routinization and dependability of responses in exchange for specific actions. As much was said by Nietzsche in *The Genealogy of Morals* when he stated that "The task of breeding an animal entitled to make promises involves, . . . the preparatory task of rendering man up to a certain point regular, uniform, equal among equals, calculable."[1] This is not to say that one cannot attempt to live beyond calculability, but only that civil society generally demands regularity. In fact, it is the apparent lack of regularity, uniformity, and calculability that unsettles many groups in today's civil society. In response to this situation, some embattled social groups have mobilized in an attempt to combat disruptive and uncalculable social relations.

The Promise Keepers are an interesting social phenomenon partly because they question the benefit and often openly reject the utility of governmental involvement in solving disruptive social conditions. By de-emphasizing participation in the political process and stressing social action on the level of individual responsibility, the Promise Keepers are attempting to change the relationships that threaten their civil society. In doing so, they are promoting social policies that some political and social activists have been advocating for years, including building strong marriages and families, removing racial barriers, and committing to moral and ethical standards. In many ways, the Promise Keepers are combating the perceived decline in the values that provide the foundation for community and civil society, a development recent commentators have referred to as America's declining social capital. By focusing on the individual's relationship with others, the Promise Keepers can be interpreted as the architects of social capital and as champions of the recently popular, but overdetermined phrase, "family values."

This chapter investigates the relationships between social capital, civil society, morality, and individualism by providing a "parochial" level of analysis of the Promise Keepers movement. I hesitate to call the men "members" because there are no administrative requirements that must be met or financial dues that must be paid in order to belong to Promise Keepers; Promise Keepers is more of an identification than a mass organization. Most men identify themselves as "promise keepers" rather than members of an organization called Promise Keepers, but more on this later.

A parochial level of analysis investigates the Promise Keepers through the intimate relationships they form with immediate members of their community. On the one hand, this approach to the Promise Keepers is parochial because it is narrowly restricted to the relationships they form with their wives, children, and other Promise Keepers, "brothers" as they are called. On the other hand, this approach is parochial in the sense that these relationships mediate and are constitutive of the formation of social capital and provide sustenance for a community of "parishioners." A parish is an administrative element of the religious and civil structures of a community. It is the locus where religious and civil values are exchanged between individuals of a social order, facilitating the formation of a community. Hence, a parishioner is someone who is always already constituting and constituent of a religious/civil order. It is in the mediation of these parochial moments, in a community of parishioners, that social capital can be forged. This level of analysis not only has implications for understanding civil society, but also may contribute to delineating the theoretical implications of social capital and individualism in a civil society perceived to be embattled by moral relativism.

## Communitarian Theory and Social Capital

In order to discuss the utilitarian aspects of social capital in (re)building civil society, a general discussion of the theory behind the concept is necessary. One can trace the theoretical roots of social capital to communitarian theory's concern with the workings of a functional community. Social capital is an assertion about the utility of individuals coming together in a group to accomplish things they could not accomplish on their own. In its simplest form, social capital is defined by the actions it facilitates. An example would be individual A trusting individual B, often with B reciprocating A's trust, which facilitates A's (and possibly B's) present and future activities. Social capital operates in those instances when an individual is enabled through immediate social relations to contribute to civil society in ways he would be unable to contribute without the support and norms of a social group. Social capital is an attempt to conceptualize the practical and generally mundane, and yet extraordinarily peculiar, aspects of civil society.

Social capital is only the most recent hybrid of communitarian theory's unquestioned belief in the individual's conditional relation to social function. The specific form of social function will vary over time, but the necessity of social function is never abated. The form varies, ranging from structural concerns with authority or the role of citizenship, to ethical issues such as trust and responsibility. Within the varying forms, however, is a longstanding theoretical assumption regarding the functional dynamics of the individual.

Robert Nisbet's *The Quest for Community* was a post-World War II example of communitarian theory's focus on functionalism. Nisbet emphasized the degeneration of the "individual's relation to social *function* and social *authority*."[2] He criticized autonomous individualism, characterizing it as a "tragically irrelevant, even intolerable" theory of civic freedom.[3] Nisbet's critique was based on a judgment that individualism had become inadequate as a "philosophy of means," because it could no longer deliver the freedom its defenders had long promised.[4] For Nisbet, modern individualism led to alienation, frustration, and loneliness rather than to its proclaimed goals of autonomy and personal choice. The alienated, frustrated, and isolated individual, disassociated from a small supportive social group, was susceptible to totalitarian political intimidation and threatened the functioning of a modern free society.

Nisbet was convinced that a thriving civil society was only possible if based on small social groups. Within the context of the small group, the individual gained the requisite personality necessary to function in relation to societal authority. Nisbet argued that the consolidation of function and authority in the totalitarian state augured the loss of a genuinely free society. His solution was to reinvigorate civil society through the individual's association with small social groups. Nisbet argued that "Social groups, . . . thrive only when they possess significant functions and authorities in the lives of their members."[5] His point was that civil society should no longer attempt to "create the conditions within which autonomous *individuals* could prosper," but that civil society should strive to "create the conditions within which autonomous *groups* may prosper."[6]

Nisbet's justification for the promotion of small social groups provides an important point of view for any contemporary discussion of social capital, but it often provides a less than explicit discussion of the moral underpinnings of civil society. Recent social critiques have filled this void. One prominent example is Robert Bellah et al., *Habits of the Heart.* In *Habits of the Heart* there is a candid discussion of the moral foundations of modern individualism. Bellah shares Nisbet's suspicions regarding the effectiveness of individualism to provide freedom in civil society, arguing that individualism has become cancerous to any freedom seeking community.[7] But whereas Nisbet was concerned with tempering the excesses of individualism with the resources of the small social group, Bellah is more interested in moderating individualism by grounding it in civic republicanism and biblical tradition. Bellah believes that "only the civic and biblical forms of individualism - forms that see the individual in relation to a larger whole, a community and a tradition - are capable of sustaining genuine individuality and nurturing both public and private life."[8] Bellah is still concerned with the individual's relation to social function, since he wants to make an individual's inner moral debate public discourse, but he pays little attention to an individual's relation to social authority. Perhaps this is because if a member of society is invested with civic republicanism and biblical tradition there will be few unanswered questions concerning social authority.

Bellah's prescription for reconstituting the social world was not a reactionary return to the raw functionalism of tradition, but a more subtle reformulation of the importance of civic republicanism and biblical tradition for a culture seemingly dominated by self-cultivation. Bellah offers several strategies for accomplishing cultural revival, but a fundamental first step is to re-emphasize and recapture the necessity of "communities of memory."[9] Bellah argues any real community is a community "that does not forget its past."[10] It is in a community's constitutive narrative, in the stories it tells itself, that "it offers examples of the men and women who have embodied and exemplified the meaning of the community."[11] Communities of memory not only bind the individual to a distant past, but also construct hope through the examples of the heroes and traditions they choose to honor. Grounded in tradition, while honoring and cherishing its fundamental republican and biblical values, Bellah foresees an individualism constituted and protected by the community. He argues for an individuality constituted through the functionalism of social exchange and sheltered by the morals and values of civic republicanism and biblical tradition. This form of individualism would no longer be susceptible to the totalitarian intimidation that Nisbet had feared, but would foster individuals who would be dependable and calculable members of a community.

Whereas Nisbet was most concerned with the structural aspects of community and Bellah was preoccupied with its moral (cultural) underpinnings, one can argue that Robert Putnam's notion of social capital is a theoretical hybrid of the two earlier reflections. Putnam combines Nisbet's structuralism with Bellah's moralism to form a functionalism based on associative moral communication, and calls the product social capital. Putnam defines social capital as the "features of social life - networks, norms, and trust - that enable participants to act together more effectively to pursue shared objectives."[12] The examples he provides in his definition include both the structural focus of Nisbet and the ethical dimension of Bellah. The networks Putnam refers to are the small social groups where the individual gains the requisite personality necessary to function in relation to societal authority. The norms and trust are Putnam's effort to ground associative activity in a moral and ethical order. Social capital becomes the combination and mediation of the structural and moral qualities that undergird a community, the qualities that bind the individual to a structural moral order.

According to Putnam's analysis, social capital in America has been declining since the 1950s. He argues that individuals are spending more time disassociated from other members of their community. A distilled example of Putnam's thesis is that more people than ever are bowling, but that fewer and fewer people are bowling in leagues.[13] This may appear to be a simple and inconsequential finding, but Putnam suggests that it is a symptom of a greater crisis in civic engagement. Similarly to Nisbet, Putnam argues that it is in small social groups like bowling leagues, card clubs, or church choirs that individuals form the networks that may lead to further civic associations. He is not arguing that civic engagement should be modeled on American bowling leagues, but that bowling leagues and other small social groups provide an opportunity for the development of sustained and functional networks of social activity.

But this is not yet a full theoretical examination of the social capital framework. In fact, it is only the "social" part. The "capital" metaphor becomes less analytical the further one delves into its communitarian foundations. If small social groups provide an opportunity for civic engagement, then it is the attendant norms and trust that provide the sustenance necessary for building "good" social capital. But this raises an interesting question; can there be "bad" social capital? If, for example, one discusses a corporation's capital assets, it is relatively clear that capital is the material wealth and assets of the corporation that can be used to create more wealth and assets. CEOs and business leaders often make distinctions between "good" and "bad" capital, but their distinction is generally based on the bottom line, their profit margin. Some have argued that this is not always the case, since moral and ethical issues may influence and determine business decisions. For example, a publishing house may choose to print innocuous travel guides instead of racy pornographic materials on the grounds of moral considerations rather than economic motives. Notwithstanding such debates, one would not expect the publishing house to argue that their printing presses were anything less than a capital asset. In other words, there may be some disagreement and discussion of the utility, durability, or condition of a capital asset, and perhaps a concurrent moral discussion of how it is used, but for the most part an asset remains an asset.

But a discussion of social capital is far less transparent. It is easy to conjure up an idyllic image of people coming together in a small social group to participate in a social activity that may lead to a sustained civic engagement. But what if this small group is an innercity gang? Or perhaps a militia? Would not this also be an opportunity for the development of social capital? Putnam agrees that it would be an opportunity, stating that "groups like the Michigan militia or youth gangs also embody *a kind of* social capital, for these networks and norms, too, enable members to cooperate more effectively," but he goes on to conclude that this form of social capital may be "to the detriment of the wider community."[14] Putnam does not seem to be concerned with the fact, or chooses to ignore it, that his form of "good" social capital may be a detriment to the militia community or to gang members. This is where the concept of capital loses it economic transparency and becomes a question of morality.

The identification of the particular norms that facilitate people working together is an example of the economic model of capital applied to an investigation of community. But when it becomes obvious to Putnam that particular kinds of social capital are less than desirable, he no longer discusses norms such as trust and respect in a productive context, but has traversed into a moral and ethical discussion of what particular groups might produce with the norms of trust and respect. The distinction is important and subtle; the first is the application of the economic concept of capital to an investigation of social relations, while the second becomes a critique and advocation of how those "capital" assets should be used. Putnam does not criticize the militias for building social capital within their groups, but for the harm they supposedly could inflict on the greater community (i.e., Bellah). The capital in Putnam's social capital is an underdetermined term with its morality hidden in socio-econometrics. In other words, social capital is a loaded concept, an always already present morality wrapped with communitarian integuments.

Should this come as a surprise? Not if one is interested in building a dependable moral community, as Putnam appears to be. The problem with social capital is that it seductively presents itself as a socio-econometrics while omitting its moral propensity. Whereas Bellah had advocated the reconstruction of communities of memory, Putnam appears to be willing to forget (ignore) the precipitous and difficult work of distilling the moral requirements for the community of memory (the "good" society). It is in Putnam's presumption of the obviousness of his moral concerns that the metaphor of social capital begins to lose its analytical clarity and becomes akin to traditional social critiques.

But does this mean social capital is a useless and inappropriate concept for studying the Promise Keepers? Can one still discern analytical clarity from Putnam's social capital without being ensnared by its moral integuments? The answer to the first question is no, as in fact, the concept becomes even more cogent with its communitarian and moral integuments exposed. The answer to the second question is less clear. If one is interested in purging social capital of its moral integuments, one would have to disengage the values from the structures. For example, an investigation of the norm of trust would have to be studied apart from its functional role in a social relation (structure). The act of "trusting" would have to be taken away from the individuals who trust. This would be necessary because social function is itself a normative value declaration. But if one can understand that functionalism has attendant moral integuments, then a workable and morally unabashed social capital can help to clarify the ideological practices used by individuals and social groups. This does not imply an affinity for or defense of a particular ideological practice, but rather an effort to clarify the type of morality inherent in functionalism. Social capital cannot be purged of its moral integuments without ensuing to theoretical abstractions.

Putnam's social capital and the Promise Keepers movement have become popular at relatively the same time because they both offer individuals a project of building a meaningful and well ordered civil society in a period seemingly devoid of meaning and morals. Both offer willing individuals a chance to form a social order in accordance with their frame of reference. But whereas Putnam is unable or unwilling to fully embrace social capital's moral integuments, the Promise Keepers have no such inability as evidenced by the Seven Promises of a Promise Keeper (see Appendix). The Seven Promises provide a lucid and morally explicit compendium on how to build social capital. They are a litany of structural and moral conditions that men can apply to rebuild their community and personal lives, to build what Putnam might call "*a kind of*" social capital.

The kind of social capital the Promise Keepers are building is devoutly and candidly colored with morality. Perhaps that is why their message attracts and resonates with so many men. The Promise Keepers message of building networks and norms of social associations does not take the form of an academic discussion of the good society, but rather is a potent and specific program for action. The Promise Keepers know what Putnam is unable to proclaim. They have the moral mandate that Putnam is unwilling to delineate. They are devout and revivalistic whereas Putnam can only be coy and academic.

The following section details what a workable, that is morally explicit, social capital looks like. In investigating the Promise Keepers, the revised and workable social capital is based on an understanding that its analytical clarity is enveloped in an always already present Christian morality. This does not dismiss social capital as an analytical device, but places it in the hands of individuals who are not only eager to implement its structural fundamentals (the building of dependable social relations), but who are also willing to embrace and abide by its moral integuments.

## Civil Society, Men of Integrity, and Social Capitalists

> What matters is the frame of reference. If, for one reason or another, the individual's immediate society comes to seem remote, purposeless, and hostile, if a people come to sense that, together, they are victims of discrimination and exclusion, not all the food and jobs in the world will prevent them from looking for the kind of surcease that comes with membership in a social and moral order seemingly directed toward their very souls.
>
> Robert A. Nisbet, *Quest for Community*

Robert Nisbet is describing a civil society that has failed to provide for the spiritual needs of many of its members. The untended members do not lack food, employment, or other material benefits; what they lack is the social tranquillity and belonging provided by small social groups. From their frame of reference, the tranquil civil society they were raised to believe in has been replaced by disorder and agitation. They no longer feel they belong to or are accepted by their own social order. Nisbet is not discussing American civil society in the 1990s, although it seems that many people would accept his depiction as quite in tune with today's social situation. Nisbet is attempting to explain the seduction and appeal of a supposedly quite dissimilar social order, communism. His point is that civil society must provide more than just material fulfillment, it must also furnish a purposeful faith in something stable, good, and worthy of sacrifice. Nisbet suggests that when the esteemed beliefs of a civil society become relative to all other values, a social order loses its moral mandate and its members lose their faith in the civil society.

It is not the point of emphasis in this section to analyze the theories and evidence that might support or refute communitarian theory's depiction of civil society, but it is important to understand that this is what the Promise Keepers believe. They believe that modern civil society is bereft of higher moral values. They feel abused and harassed for their beliefs. Their frame of reference depicts a civil society overrun by moral relativism, no longer a place where traditional values are traditionally validated. From their frame of reference, vice reigns over virtue, indifference over judgment, and promise making over promise keeping. Succumbing to temptation is popularized as something everyone is doing, while adherence to a moral, ethical, or sexual standard is criticized as judgmental and as exhibiting a lack of understanding. Fitting in and not hurting anyone's feelings becomes the golden rule, while maintaining one's convictions and integrity is portrayed as antagonistic and insensitive. It matters little if this is a fair and accurate depiction of contemporary civil society. Perspectives are rarely fair and even less often accurate. What is important is that from their frame of reference, from the way the Promise Keepers experience civil society, it is more often than not an uncivil society.

But if civil society appears to be uncivil from the Promise Keepers frame of reference, what course of action do they propose and recommend? In other words, what do the Promise Keepers believe it would take to transform what they perceive to be an uncivil social order into a stable and civil society?

One starting point is to investigate a theme found in both the discourse on social capital and the texts and narratives of the Promise Keepers movement. This common theme is integrity. The Promise Keepers logo is a large 'PK' followed by the phrase "Men of Integrity." Integrity is defined as a consistent adherence to a standard of values. Something with integrity is thought to be sound and undivided, complete. In regard to the Promise Keepers, integrity is the ability to keep your word. It is the ability to "let your 'Yes' be 'Yes' and your 'No' be 'No.'"[15]

Integrity is an interesting word in that it refers both to a function or quality of being and to a state of being. As a function, integrity adheres an individual to a standard of values. In this case, integrity functions as the linchpin between the individual and the standard of values. As the individual is confronted by an activity, or when he is evaluating some previous sequence of events, he can measure his actions against the table of values. If what he is proposing to do (or has done) measures up to his standard of values, then his activities are legitimated by the code. If the activity does not correspond to the standard, and if the individual wants to think of himself as a man of integrity, then the proposed activity will not be performed. A simple example would be a married man confronted with an adulterous liaison. Most marriage commitments, whether legal or spiritual, view adultery as a violation of the integrity of the marriage. A man of integrity, when confronted by his sexual desires, will seek counsel in his standard of values. If he has given his word to sexual fidelity in a marriage vow, then he will avoid the adulterous liaison and maintain his standard of values. (If a man no longer knows what the proper standard of values is, he can refer to the Seven Promises of the Promise Keepers.) By keeping his word, the tempted man has used his promises to create social capital. Since his 'Yes' means 'Yes,' and his 'No' means 'No,' his word becomes a reliable commodity that can be exchanged with other men of integrity.

Integrity as a state of being highlights the necessary role of the act of integrity in producing the subject of integrity. In Nietzschian terms, the doing produces the doer. The state of being a man of integrity posits the individual as complete and stable. The individual is reconciled to the code of values. His being becomes whole, complete, and dependable. He becomes a promise keeper with an identity reconciled to his actions. His identity (a concept) is hypostatized through his actions (the concrete), thus providing a foundation for further activity.

As I noted at the beginning of this chapter, the Promise Keepers describe our current times as an "age of moral relativism." The foreword to their 1996 study guide, *Promise Builders Study Series: Applying the Seven Promises*, states that "Our society says it really doesn't matter what you do as long as *you* believe in it - and don't restrict others from doing the same."[16] In the same book, in a section discussing Daniel's deliverance from the lions, Bill McCartney is quoted exhorting men to be more like Daniel, to be men of integrity:

> Don't be like the chameleon who fits into every situation. When he's with the people in the church, he's churchlike. But when he's with the guys in the street, he's like one of the guys in the street. Come out from among them. Show them the contradiction; show them the alternative; show them how a Promise Keeper lives![17]

According to the Promise Keepers, men of integrity are not chameleons. They are also not moral relativists. They know the true standard of values and are called forth to implement that standard in their daily lives. They understand that by "living in a culture dominated by sensuality," they are also tempted by immorality.[18] But the man of integrity, with his faith firmly in the Lord, can conquer the age of moral relativism and change the relationships that undergird civil society. The Promise Keepers focus on the little things, claiming that both God and Satan can be found in the little events in their daily lives. Satan is a distracter, a force that leads men down the immoral path. Satan attempts to chip away at a man's integrity, telling him that all views are to be accepted, all people are okay, or that his little sins do not really hurt anyone.

By focusing on the little things, the Promise Keepers provide men with a place to begin building social capital, to become architects of social capital. Through their focus on the little things, a researcher can make a distinction between at least two types of Promise Keepers who build social capital. The first is the Promise Keeper who is externally concerned with moral relativism in his community. Instead of political efficacy, one could say this kind of Promise Keeper exhibits social efficacy. He feels he can change civil society, is an activist, and sees himself as part of a larger social movement. He is an activist looking for an agenda. This "external social capitalist" views the Promise Keepers movement as the logical response of men who no longer feel a part of social order. His characteristics generally include a longstanding relationship with Jesus, a successful (re-)marriage, and a feeling of social efficacy. His overriding view is revivalistic, with Promise Keepers as a manifestation of the coming Christian renewal.

The second type of Promise Keeper provides a subtle but influential form of social capital because he "personalizes" the capital he is building. This is not to say that the externally directed social capitalist does not personalize his capital, but rather that the second kind of Promise Keeper is experiencing the process in a transforming way. Promise Keepers is something "new," an addition to his life rather than a conduit or avenue of expression for things he was already feeling. The second type of Promise Keeper is experiencing the transformation of civil society at its most parochial and immediate level, through the relationships formed with those closest to him. This kind of Promise Keeper does not see himself involved in a social movement, but is constituting a life strategy. This perspective was succinctly summarized by Richard Stone, a Promise Keeper Ambassador from Lafayette, Indiana who said "Promise Keepers is not a social movement, it's a way of life." This type of internal social capitalist is mobilized in terms of the immediate and personal benefits he is receiving through the identification and life practice of being someone who keeps his promises.

The Promise Keepers believe in social capital, although they do not use that term; they believe that if we all honored our commitments it would lead to a better society for all. When Bill McCartney was asked to envision a society 25 years from now in which men had striven to keep the Seven Promises of a Promise Keeper, he saw "a new generation of godly fathers, healthy marriages, and sturdy families setting a biblical standard for a searching world."[19] He envisions a social order rebuilt on social capital. The Promise Keepers appear to accept the definition of social capital discussed above, that social capital is the "features of social life - networks, norms, and trust - that enable participants to act together more effectively to pursue shared objectives."[20] The Promise Keepers believe that in order to (re)build the networks, norms, and trust that enable individuals to participate in society, men have to accept their biblical leadership within the family and begin adhering to a standard of values that will break the cycle of moral relativism.

## The Seven Promises, Relationships, and Brokenness

> If you were to describe Promise Keepers in one word, it would be relationship. The seven promises all speak of relationships - to God, spouse, children, pastor and church, others, and God's word.
>
> Promise Keepers, *Man of His Word Bible*

The Promise Keepers believe that in order to break the cycle of moral relativism, a man of integrity must forge relationships with others based on the values and traditions of the Bible. But forging relationships is at least a two part process, involving the individual and an (reciprocating) other. The Promise Keepers realize, in a similar manner to Bellah and others, that any practical discussion of relationships must take into account the character and disposition of individuals. Where such discussions diverge and distinguish themselves is in how they attempt to remedy and/or restrict specific manifestations of individualism. The man of integrity discussed in the previous section is an example of the manifestation of a kind of individualism recommended by the Promise Keepers. But that discussion did not outline how one becomes a man of integrity. In other words, what practices are necessary in order to make of oneself a Promise Keeper?

The making of a Promise Keeper is a two stage process involving the production of a particular kind of individualism, a man of integrity, who can then facilitate the functioning of civil society. The Seven Promises of the Promise Keepers provide a synopsis of how one goes about making a man of integrity. It is important to recall that integrity refers to both a function or quality of being and to a state of being. The Seven Promises reflect both aspects of integrity; the first three promises focus on integrity as a function of being and the last four reflect integrity as a state of being. This distinction will be further developed below, but for now it is important to note that each promise works either to adhere a man to a moral standard or to enable his development as a social capitalist and architect of civil society.

According to a 1996 book from the Promise Keepers, *Go the Distance: The Making of a Promise Keeper*, the "starting point for all meaningful change" is "*brokenness.*"[21] Brokenness is "the path of surrender, of sacrifice, of realizing we have no rights as Christians."[22] It is the surrender of one's pride, a commitment to self-sacrifice, and the realization that one has no rights outside God's will. Brokenness is the "nonnegotiable prerequisite" for becoming a man of integrity.[23] Brokenness breaks the individual of his pride and selfishness, interpellating him as one who needs the Lord. Instead of attempting to fulfill the self through his own will (autonomous individualism), the Promise Keeper realizes the futility of the effort and proclaims and embraces his brokenness, trading his irreconcilable self for an eternal relationship with God. According to the Promise Keepers, the surrender is not a sacrifice, but rather a gift of hope and meaning. In brokenness they find hope for a better (more godly) world.

But why is brokenness the "nonnegotiable prerequisite" for becoming a man of integrity? Why must one be broken in order to be a Promise Keeper? How does brokenness affect the potential of a man to become a builder of social capital? It is in brokenness that men are enabled. In brokenness they can begin to think of their personal relationships in terms other than the contractual orientation of creditor and debtor. In accepting Jesus Christ, their debt is transferred to a metaphysical banker, who in return provides the broken man with an endless supply of credit. The broken man is freed of the bonds of typical social relations because he no longer selfishly works for the other in the relationship, but only serves the Lord. Only by giving up their pride and selfish desires can men then become men of integrity, men who can keep their promises, men who no longer run from their commitments. The broken man is the man who can potentially let his 'Yes' be 'Yes' and his 'No' be 'No' because he has transcended the sins of the ego. The broken man, the man free of pride and selfishness, is a man who can keep his word.

The broken man is a potential man of integrity only after he has formed a relationship with Jesus. The first promise of a Promise Keeper is to be "committed to honoring Jesus Christ through worship, prayer, and obedience to God's Word in the power of the Holy Spirit" (Seven Promises in the Appendix). Just by being broken, without the hope and protection of Jesus, a man is lost in anomie and can never become a consistent promise keeper. Accepting Jesus is the first step after brokenness because it allows the Promise Keeper to attempt to reflect the image of Jesus in this world. But Jesus also functions as a sort of guardian or steward in a turbulent world. As a hypostasis, as the uniting of divine and human natures, Jesus performs the role of a "concierge,"[24] standing guard at the door to the broken man's world. The concierge lives in the building (in this case the body), attends the entrance (in this case the psyche), and serves as a janitor (in this case unsoiling the sinner). The concierge keeps pride and selfishness from entering the psyche, disabling their promises of rapture and fulfillment.

Jesus functions in the same way as a concierge by standing in the doorway of self-reflection. His function is to interpellate the individual into a promise keeper even when there is no sovereign (civil) authority watching. The man who has accepted his brokenness and forged a relationship with Jesus will no longer succumb to moral relativism. He will no longer be "overcome by the temptation to compromise his convictions."[25] He may still fail, succumb to pride and selfishness, and break his promises, but he will now know the difference between a life of promise keeping and a life of promise breaking. Alone with his concierge, he will have a better chance of resisting the temptation to look at *Sports Illustrated*'s new swimsuit edition, to order the X-rated movie on the pay-per-view, or to surf the net in search of adult entertainment. With his concierge he can strive to be a man of integrity, a man of his word, and an architect of social capital.

In striving to build the kind of individualism that enables a man of integrity, the Promise Keepers also feel it is necessary for a man to have a close support group of likeminded men. The second promise of a Promise Keeper is a commitment "to pursuing vital relationships with a few other men, understanding that he needs brothers to help him keep his promises." These few other men, brothers as they are called,[26] are necessary for support, encouragement, and accountability. The commitment to pursue vital relationships with other men is an acknowledgment that traditional forms of individualism have often left men lonely, disconnected, and susceptible to temptation. The formation of vital relations with other men is an effort to transform the culturally constructed "lone ranger" mystique and to replace it with a biblically oriented man of fellowship and mentoring.

After the broken man accepts Jesus as his concierge and commits to pursuing vital relationships with other men, he becomes a potential man of integrity. The third promise completes the triangulation of a functionally enabling individualism. It is a commitment "to practicing spiritual, moral, ethical, and sexual purity." This is the integrity promise, a commitment to life practices that act as the linchpin between an individual and a standard of values. Almost every book published and endorsed by the Promise Keepers focuses on a man's relationship with Jesus, his brothers, and his adherence to a biblical standard of value. The third promise provides a standard against which to measure one's life practices. It is a promise that is intended to draw men back to a biblical understanding of spiritual, moral, ethical, and sexual purity, while at the same time augmenting a defense against situational ethics and moral relativism. A description of this perceived dearth of purity is summarized in one of the short essays in *Seven Promises of a Promise Keeper*. Gary Oliver, a contributor to the book, states the following:

> Thirty-five years ago, our country followed the Judeo-Christian ethic. Few people questioned that chastity was a good thing, that hard work was the duty of every responsible man, that homosexual conduct was wrong, and that it was never right to lie, cheat, steal, or commit adultery. But today, our ethics and morals are no longer based on Jerusalem; they're based on Sodom and Gomorrah.[27]

Oliver goes on to offer a seven step program to help a man maintain his integrity in a culture based on the values of Sodom and Gomorrah. In this seven step program, the individual must make a commitment not to be influenced by current social morality, to live God's word, and to avoid beguiling social situations. Oliver's seven step program also enjoins the individual to guard his heart, mind, and eyes, while remaining vigilant toward the little things in life.[28] This would be a remarkable undertaking for any individual, but it is relevant to a discussion of social capital because it typifies the kind of recommendations and advice provided by the Promise Keepers. The first three parts of the program ask men to bring a biblical standard of value into their daily lives in order to avoid

the abyss called contemporary civil society. The second three parts remind men that they are vulnerable (sinful) individuals and that they must not separate themselves from the protection provided by a concierge, brothers, and a moral standard. The final point is a reminder that they must remain vigilant toward the little things that dominate daily life. In essence, this seven step program is an outline for the maintenance of a specific form of individualism that can produce what would be acceptable social capital to the Promise Keepers. This form of individualism, with its attendant concierge and commitment to integrity, is designed to produce calculable and responsible men of integrity.

When combined with the previous two promises, the commitment to a standard of integrity provides a consistent frame of reference from which one can measure all decisions and temptations. The enabling triangle of concierge, brothers, and a standard of value ensconces the individual Promise Keeper and protects him from immoral cultural and social influences. The triangulation has the added effect of reconciling the Promise Keepers identity to his social function, as he becomes a Christian brother with a natural moral constitution.

The first three promises construct and secure a particular form of individualism, triangulating the individual in a system of divine authority, group accountability, and spiritual, ethical, moral, and sexual purity. The remaining promises detail how this triangulated man is to deploy his integrity in relationships to build "good" social capital. The final four promises reflect a concentric social orientation, beginning with a man's family and extending out to include his church, other brothers, and the greater community. These remaining promises commit a Promise Keeper to:

1. Building strong marriages and families;

2. Supporting the mission of his church;

3. Reaching beyond any racial and denominational barriers;

4. And influencing his world, being obedient to the Great Commandment and the Great Commission.

Each promise describes an everwidening social horizon in which a Promise Keeper can become a social capitalist and architect of civil society. From the Promise Keepers perspective, by serving his wife he facilitates the family, a mutually beneficial and socially fundamental element of civil society. By participating in the lives of his children and remaining responsible for their moral and spiritual development, he is socializing the next generation of productive citizens. His commitment to supporting the mission of his church renews and empowers a vital institution within the community. His promise to reach beyond racial and denominational barriers is characterized as an opportunity to construct an everwidening and inclusive community, while also tackling one of America's most divisive social issues, race. And finally, his commitment to love his neighbor as himself (Great Commandment) and to spread Christ's message of love and salvation throughout communities and nations (Great Commission) is described by the Promise Keepers as an immeasurable potentiality for the development of civil society.[29]

The potential fulfillment of all four promises, however, is predicated on the formation of a particular form of individualism. In the Promise Keepers discourse, only the triangulated individual (with his concierge, brothers, and standard of value) is capable of constructing and maintaining the norms and networks of social capital the Promise Keepers deem necessary for the proper functioning of civil society.

## Concluding Thought

It seems fairly evident that the Promise Keepers are attempting to build norms and networks that facilitate the functioning of civil society. In this essay, I have portrayed the Promise Keepers as modern day social capitalists. This is a term they do not have in their lexicon, but one that resonates with their evangelical and communitarian spirit. With the focus on the concept of integrity and its functional role in social capital, this chapter has also attempted to trace the differing dimensions of integrity and how it is discussed by Promise Keepers. It is interesting to note how easily integrity is accepted by the movement, and how uncompromising integrity can be. A man of integrity may be dependable, faithful, and a good social capitalist, but he may also be obstinate and inflexible, characteristics that are "non-chameleon" and perhaps less than democratic.

## Notes

1. Friedrich Nietzsche, *The Birth of Tragedy and The Genealogy of Morals,* trans. Francis Golffing (New York: Anchor Books, Doubleday, 1990), 190. (Original work published 1887.)

2. Robert A. Nisbet, *Community and Power (formerly The Quest for Community)* (New York: A Galaxy Book, 1962), xi. (Italics are in the original.)

3. Ibid., 245.

4. Ibid., 245.

5. Ibid., 247.

6. Ibid., 278.

7. Robert N. Bellah, Richard Madsen, William M. Sullivan, Ann Swidler, and Steven M. Tipton, *Habits of the Heart: Individualism and Commitment in American Life* (Berkeley: University of California Press, 1985), vii.

8. Ibid., 143.

9. Ibid., 152-155. See also Alasdair McIntyre, *After Virtue* (South Bend, IN: University of Notre Dame Press, 1981), chapter 15.

10. Ibid., 153.

11. Ibid., 153.

12. Robert D. Putnam, "Tuning In, Tuning Out: The Strange Disappearance of Social Capital in America," *PS: Political Science & Politics* (December 1995), 664-665.

13. Robert D. Putnam, "Bowling Alone: America's Declining Social Capital," *Journal of Democracy*, vol. 6, no. 1 (1995), 65-78.

14. Putnam, "Tuning In, Tuning Out," 665. (Italics added.)

15. Promise Keepers Conference Program, Chicago IL (1996), 6. See also Matthew 5:37.

16. Bob Horner, Ron Ralston, and David Sunde, *Promise Builders Study Series: Applying the Seven Promises* (Colorado Springs: Focus on the Family Publishing, 1996), 5.

17. Ibid., 39. See also Daniel 6:1-28.

18. Ibid., 64.

19. Bill McCartney, "God Is Calling Us to a Higher Love," in *Go The Distance: The Making of a Promise Keeper,* ed. John Trent (Colorado Springs, CO: Focus on the Family Publishing, 1996), 7.

20. Putnam, "Tuning In, Tuning Out," 664-665.

21. Randy Phillips, "Foreword," in *Go The Distance: The Making of a Promise Keeper,* ed. John Trent (Colorado Springs: Focus on the Family Publishing, 1996), 3.

22. McCartney, "God Is Calling Us to a Higher Love," 7.

23. Ibid., 12.

24. Nietzsche, *The Birth of Tragedy and The Genealogy of Morals,* 189. Nietzsche described the concierge as the one who "maintains order and etiquette in the household of the psyche."

25. Horner, Ralston, and Sunde, *Promise Builders Study Series,* 24.

26. Geoff Gorsuch, with Dan Schaffer, *BROTHERS! Calling Men Into Vital Relationships: A Small Group Discussion Guide* (Colorado Springs: NavPress, 1994), 13.

27. Gary J. Oliver, "Black-and-White Living in a Gray World," in *Seven Promises of A Promise Keeper*, ed. Al Jannsen and Larry K. Weeden (Colorado Springs: Focus on the Family Publishing, 1994), 84.

28. Ibid., 85-90.

29. See also Ken Abraham, *Who Are the Promise Keepers?: Understanding the Christian Men's Movement* (New York: Doubleday, 1997), 34-35.

# Chapter Four

---

## For Men Only: Jesus, Nature, and Signature Moments

> While Jezebel was killing off the Lord's prophets, Obadiah had taken a hundred prophets and hidden them in two caves, fifty in each, and had supplied them with bread and water.
>
> 1 Kings 18:4

> . . . unable to make themselves into men, the women make us into women.
>
> Rousseau, *Politics and the Arts*

It was a bright Friday morning as my father and I drove from the suburbs to the church on the south side of Chicago. My father is president of the church board at a small rural congregation in northwestern Illinois. Although he is not a Promise Keeper, my father was my pretext for going to the Promise Keepers' *Pastors and Worship Leaders' Gathering for Men*, since the gathering was "open to all men on a church staff."[1]

Since gender is an underlying principle of any social order, it is important to understand how it is being constructed by the Promise Keepers. Promise Keepers is a dynamic and diverse Christian men's organization. How the Promise Keepers construct, secure, and justify gender identities is a significant factor for understanding the movement as a whole.

The Apostolic Faith Church on Chicago's south side hosted the preconference gathering. The church is located at 3823 South Indiana in the midst of some of Chicago's most notorious neighborhoods. The church itself is the only building in the neighborhood without the inner city markings of taggers and gang members. It appears as an oasis in the middle of what can only be described as a war zone. Every building in the neighborhood is either abandoned to window-smashing youths or defended with bars by stoic elders. It is not only a physical war zone, but like all contested areas, it exteriorizes conflict about ideas. The church provides a stark backdrop for the tension permeating the neighborhood because it conveys contentment in a world of discontent.

The pastors' and church leaders' gathering is designed as an opportunity for some of the leadership of the Promise Keepers to explain what they have to offer to church leaders at the local level. The gathering is presented as a time for Christian leaders to learn of "Promise Keepers' vision to strengthen pastors, worship leaders and the ministry of the local church."[2] This format was not unique to the 1996 Chicago stadium event, attended by more than 60,000 men; the gatherings seem to precede all the stadium conferences produced by the Promise Keepers. This particular meeting was attended by about 150 men; approximately one-half of the men were from minority congregations.

The Promise Keepers discussed the classic roles of a pastor in leading worship, proclaiming the Lord's Kingdom, and preaching hope. It was their intention to allay the fears that any church leaders might have had concerning the Promise Keepers. In the Christian community, there is a degree of anxiety regarding the Promise Keepers. Some congregational and denominational leaders have expressed a concern that the Promise Keepers may be detracting from the traditional roles of the church. The speakers emphasized that the Promise Keepers support and are committed to the traditional institutions within the various churches and denominations. They are not out to depose the pastor and "his" place of leadership within the church, but only hope to encourage and strengthen the men's ministry within local congregations, so that the men can better serve the congregation and the pastor. According to the presentation, the movement is only concerned with (re)invigorating a men's ministry that has historically only consisted of sporadic basketball and softball leagues. The Promise Keepers speakers were resolute in their support of and dedication to pastors and priests, asking all in attendance to affirm the Promise Keepers Atlanta Convenant, a pastoral declaration of commitment based on the Seven Promises of a Promise Keeper.

The Promise Keepers do not want women at these gatherings. I do not think they would forcibly remove a woman if she was determined to attend, but that will have to remain a matter of speculation.

The Promise Keepers have a dilemma. Women are not only the wives of pastors, but in contemporary Christian culture, they are also pastors. Women have their own congregations. They are ordained ministers. They are church leaders. But they are not welcome at Promise Keepers gatherings. For a group that prides itself on tearing down the walls that keep "us" apart, particularly concerning the issues of race and denominationalism, why do the Promise Keepers construct a wall to keep "them" away?

I posed this question to Tom Johnson, a self-identified Promise Keeper and church deacon from Gary, Indiana. Tom told me that churches can ordain women if they choose to do so, but that the ordination itself does not imply the "blessing of God." He supported this line of reasoning by referring to 1 Timothy

2:12, part of Paul's letter to the young pastor Timothy. The passage states that a woman is not permitted "to teach or to have authority over a man; she must be silent."[3] Tom said that any denomination can ordain a woman, but if the act is not based on the Bible, it is not the order of God.

There was also an admonition directed toward the pastors and church leaders. Dr. Rodney L. Cooper, the National Director of Education for the Promise Keepers, and Wes Roberts, also a representative from Promise Keepers, reproached the various leaders for disregarding the "masculine context" in the day-to-day activities of congregations. The speakers described the church as a "feminine environment."[4] Cooper and Roberts made it clear that they were not against women, that they were not saying anything derogatory about women, and that they actually liked women. Women in general were not to blame. The admonition was directed toward the men who had let this happen, or who had at least let it continue as they had found it. Their lamentations were directed at righting what they described as a twentieth century wrong – "the feminization of the church." They counseled the gathering on the importance of "making the church open to and comfortable for men." The Promise Keepers hope to make the church "safe" again, a place where a man feels comfortable being himself, where Christian men can feel secure and enabled to speak their minds and fulfill their rightful place in the church.

The feminization of the church is a metonym for the overliberalization of society. The Promise Keepers are not the first men's movement to find fault with particular aspects of American culture. An early twentieth century exprofessional baseball player turned evangelical minister, Billy Sunday, located the evils of society in the men who frequented taverns and dance halls. Sunday, an active participant in the temperance movement, was renowned for his passionate calls on the evangelical tent circuit to destroy John Barleycorn, Sunday's fiendish caricature for the evils of alcohol. Sunday was the acknowledged leader of "Muscular Christianity,"[5] a male response to the perception that women had emasculated the church and the iconography of Jesus Christ. This response to the "first wave of feminism" demanded a re-masculinization of the church and Christian iconography. Sunday called for a Christianity that was a "hard muscled, pick-axed religion, a religion from the gut, tough and resilient," rather than a "dainty, sissified, lily-livered piety."[6]

Another important Muscular Christianity organization was the Men and Religion Forward Movement of 1911-12. The leaders of this movement, building on the evangelical energy of Billy Sunday, preached that "the manly gospel of Christ should be presented to men by men" and that women "have had charge of the Church work long enough."[7]

The Promise Keepers differ slightly, but with a significant theoretical implication, from Muscular Christianity. The difference is not in their call for a stronger more manly Christianity, but rather in their effort to have it both ways, to keep the emotive, traditionally feminine, Jesus, and to reaffirm a masculine Jesus. This point will be further developed below, but it is important to understand that the Promise Keepers are not just concerned with remasculinizing Christianity; they are just as concerned with maintaining and expanding Christianity's "softer" side.[8] This "softer" side is redefined as a natural masculine characteristic, complementing and not contradicting a man's "harder" side.

According to the Promise Keepers, contemporary culture is dominated by liberal influences that dismiss and denigrate the natural order reflected in biblical tradition. The modern demon is man's willingness to privilege temporal liberal values over eternal biblical tradition. But, for the Promise Keepers, this is not the way things have to be. Feminization is a process; it is a constructed state of social values as well as an artificial state of being. To be feminized, for a man, is to be less than the embodiment of biblical masculinity found in the image of Jesus Christ. The narratives and testimonials edited and produced by the Promise Keepers organization reflect both a hegemonic and nonhegemonic gender ideology, hegemonic referring to traditional gender ideology, and nonhegemonic to the Christ-based masculinity. The Christ-based ideology substitutes the symmetric reflection of Jesus Christ for the asymmetric reflection of the eternal feminine. It is a nonhegemonic ideology because it is at present subsumed by the traditional reflective gender formation of male/masculine-female/feminine. Hegemony still reigns: asymmetric gender ideology, referred to by Michael Messner in *Politics of Masculinities* as biblical essentialism, is still the dominant way of understanding gender with men who identify themselves as Promise Keepers. The Christ-based symmetric ideology is found in Promise Keepers publications and given voice by men closely affiliated with the Promise Keepers, particularly the leadership.

Feminization is used as a metonym for all that is unnatural to man. Feminization signifies liberal culture. Masculinity signifies nature. Feminization is that which distracts man from his true nature, from his biblical masculinity. One result of feminization is the person who stands for nothing and follows anything. This type of individual is described by the Promise Keepers as a "people-pleaser." Gary Smalley and John Trent, two prominent Promise Keepers, state that "many men who grow up in a feminized environment skip over independence and opt for over-dependence."[9] The people-pleaser is overdependent, or codependent, on others for validation of his or her beliefs and values. According to Smalley and Trent, this characteristic "used to be a particularly feminine ailment," but "the ranks of co-dependent men are growing rapidly."[10] This is the "sensitive man," the male who is unable to say 'no' to others. His values and beliefs are fickle and malleable; he is dependent on others for validation of what he believes, and is therefore easily seduced by cultural trends. This codependency, this "particularly feminine ailment," disables the male's ability to lead.[11] A man (leader) always looking to others for affirmation is nothing but an appeaser, a minion of popular opinion.[12]

The presentation was full of humorous and anecdotal stories of how men are different from women. The audience was told that there is a difference in how men and women approach the issue of wearing clothing. Women make clothes an event, whereas men wear them out of obligation. Women will begin planning on Tuesday what they are going to wear on Saturday. Men, on the other hand, will wear whatever happens to be clean on Saturday. This characterization was humorous to the audience; it seemed that all the men had experienced similar situations.

The audience was also told that men like their space. Men are competitive by nature and need their space in order to distance the competition. The speaker from Promise Keepers asked the audience to notice how far apart each man was sitting from the man next to him. As we all looked at each other, it was apparent that almost all the men were at least an arm's length away from the man on either side. In part, this can be explained by the size and seating capacity of the church itself; the auditorium could accommodate approximately five hundred worshipers. But the point was not missed by the audience; men feel safe at a distance and view closeness as a danger. It was then pointed out that women are just the opposite; women perceive closeness as security not danger. Women appreciate and need intimacy because they feel more secure the closer they are to someone. But traditionally, men have perceived intimacy to be a sign of vulnerability and danger.

Then Roberts discussed the need for men to grow beyond this fear and begin to see the authenticity of male intimacy, an authentic male intimacy reflective of Jesus Christ rather than characteristics traditionally defined as feminine. Intimacy is not a feminine trait; rather, intimacy is a Christ-like quality. He stressed how important it is for men to witness other men being intimate with each other in the same way that the disciples learned from Jesus. Jesus is the living image of biblical masculinity. But men will only learn from Jesus when they witness his teachings for themselves.

Michael Messner's book, *The Politics of Masculinities*, briefly examines the Promise Keepers reliance on biblical essentialism. But the concept, and its application to the Promise Keepers, can be further expanded and refined. Not only do the Promise Keepers essentialize masculinity based on anatomy, but they also secure the identification as masculine male in Christ-likeness. As will be discussed below, such an identification constructs masculinity as part of the Holy Trinity and subordinates femininity to something less than the Father, Son, and Holy Spirit.

According to Roberts, men need to see men embracing other men – not quick shoulder hugs, which are nothing more than hasty bodily squeezes, but real fullbodied embraces. They again used humor to ease the audience, pointing out that men need to be able to show their emotions in the same way as the Bud Light commercial guy, the "I Love You Man!" character. They were quick to point out, though, that "I love you man!" does not imply or lead to "I want you man!" The caveat to this desire for intimacy was a clear and concise declaration that this intimacy was nonsexual in nature. On several occasions, Roberts stated that nonsexual closeness was acceptable. Men could hold hands in prayer, embrace each other, and love each other, as long as the intimacy was confined to the realm of nonsexual behavior.[13]

The Promise Keepers construction of masculinity as any identity performance but homosexuality is illustrative of their intensifying and arresting of the body and desire. This form of masculinity asks men to intensely feel the love of man – but stop before you touch him inappropriately. Intensely love the other but beware of inappropriate desire.

Roberts went on to discuss the recent popular book by John Gray, *Men are from Mars, Women are from Venus*. This book argues that men and women think differently. Men think in terms of logic or emotion, but never both at the same time, whereas women are capable of both, simultaneously. Utilizing an analogy from Gray's book, Roberts stated that when men are confronted by a problem they go into a cave. The cave is how men get away from the world in order to think. In this cave, a man attempts to find a practical solution to the problem confronting him. If he cannot find a solution, his (natural) tendency is to "clam up," to tune the rest of the world out, and to keep others from entering his cave. This, the Promise Keepers suggested, is how the individual man confronts the problems of the world. He spends too much time alone in his cave away from his brothers. A man becomes isolated and unsettled. He loses his bearings and questions his identity. Roberts concluded his presentation by emphasizing that men can learn to find strength in emotional closeness, but only after they witness men empowered through nonsexual forms of male intimacy. Roberts reminded the audience that even in the Bible, in a time of moral decay and social unrest, men retreated to a cave for security and to escape persecution from Ahab's wife, Jezebel.

To this audience of spiritual leaders, Jezebel would signify the temptress, the licentious woman, the treacherous schemer, and the dominating wife who led Ahab, the king of northern Israel, away from his Hebrew heritage and into the service of Baal.[14] Baalism was an idolatrous and carnal cult that prospered during the reign of Ahab, primarily under the leadership of Jezebel and her family. As Ahab stood idly by, Jezebel undertook a pogrom aimed at destroying the Jewish religious culture. When Obadiah safely hid the men in the cave from Jezebel's persecution, he was not only protecting their lives, but was also safeguarding and sheltering them from a (feminized) culture of immorality and idolatry.

The implication from the Promise Keepers perspective is that men have remained alone in their caves too long and that this departure has contributed to many of society's problems, including the feminization of the church. With an evangelical spirit, the present is proclaimed as the time for action and not for retreat. It is time for men to come out of their caves and to take their rightful place of leadership within the church again.

But what kind of masculinity comes out of the cave? What does the cave symbolize? If the cave provides shelter and respite from a contentious liberal (feminized) culture, what kind of masculinity will also provide the same security and comfort that the cave does?

Some segments of the recent men's movement, in particular the mythopoetic and the Promise Keepers, attempt to locate, identify, and secure that which marks masculinity. The search for the origins of masculinity leads the mythopoetic movement to Jungian psychology and a loose essentialism based on difference and the integration of a man's anima, his inner woman.[15] The Promise Keepers, on the other hand, begin and end their search for a secure masculinity in the story of Adam in the Garden of Eden and Jesus Christ. Both accounts rely on myth, faith, metaphor, and vitally descriptive language. A secure and often dark space, similar to the cave discussed above, is consistently attributed to men and their masculinity. Robert Bly's Iron John, the archetype of the mythopoetic movement, is brought forth from the depths of a pond located deep in a forest (Adam was alone in the Garden of Eden). Iron John is found "lying on the bottom of the pond" and is described as "a large man covered with hair from head to foot."[16] Masculinity is often found in the earthly confines of the forest and the clarion call of beating drums.

The Promise Keepers do not retreat to the forest to search for their masculinity, but rather attempt to reproduce the security of the cave in a more modern male domain such as the untroubled safety of the sports stadium and the ease of a small group of men. The sports arena is a place where men can be comfortable being men. Small accountability/support groups, where men meet to discuss issues and concerns, or a men's Bible study, provide another secure environment. All of these are efforts to provide men with secure environments, places where they can feel safe being men.

But what happens when men venture out of their safety zone? What happens when man meets woman and hegemonic gender ideology confronts Promise Keepers masculinity? How do the Promise Keepers attempt to secure and safeguard masculinity in a culture fraught with femininity and feminism?

## Christ, The Masculine Imago

It is assumed that part of a man's identity is a construction of and negotiation with the question of masculinity. The Promise Keepers movement contests contemporary social constructions of gender and sexuality. Their strong stance against homosexuality, along with their promise of sexual purity (part of the third promise), enables men to exhibit and perform emotive, caring, and attentive subject positions that have been historically constructed as feminine, or at least as less than masculine. By promising sexual purity, based on heterosexuality as the standard of purity, the Promise Keepers perform a masculinity that incorporates culturally constructed feminine codes without the accusation of being any less of a man. In doing so, the Promise Keepers differ from Muscular Christianity. Muscular Christianity attempted to remasculinize Christianity. The church had become soft and needed a strong dose of masculinity. But the Promise Keepers are not *only* a retro-masculinity movement. They want to keep the "softness" while redefining it as a natural characteristic of biblical masculinity. Therefore, the Promise Keepers are able to expand their gender performance to include culturally constructed feminine traits and to reaffirm their subject position (the comfortable masculine heterosexual male) as the social norm.

The construction of the comfortable masculine heterosexual male is accomplished without a direct encounter with what it means to be feminine, therefore without contesting traditional gender ideology. Women are only alluded to as the assumed other of marriage, motherhood, and heterosexual desire. When femininity is present, as the previous discussion suggested, it is associated with culture rather than nature. Femininity no longer functions as the reliable (natural) reflexive double of masculinity in traditional gender ideology.

Traditional gender ideology functions through a lived (experienced) narrative of how one thinks of oneself in relation to others.[17] It is adjectival, always already descriptive of a noun; it is always already a descriptive ontology, in the sense that gender becomes something lived, a Stirnerian ownness if you will. For many, gender feels so natural that it is accorded the status of Nature. This creates the dilemma of any identity order based on some conception of Nature; how to account for identity performances outside of the order of Nature. Historically, those outside of the traditional binary of male/masculine-female/feminine have often been beaten, persecuted, ostracized, and even killed for living their performance. More recently, the traditional hegemonic order has been undermined (expanded?) by a limited openness and ostensible acceptance of "nonnatural" gender performances. As this happens, masculinity and femininity have been detached from a biological determination and allowed a wider range of performance.

The Promise Keepers begin their engagement of these expanded performances in the cultural *bricolage* from the position of traditional hegemonic ideology. The Promise Keepers use this paradigm as a starting point, as a way of attracting men to a comfortable and relaxed state of mind in the same way the movie "It's a Wonderful Life" conjures up an idyllic and enjoyable image of what it means to partake of society. But men involved in the Promise Keepers also experience the traditional framework of male/masculine-female/feminine in restrictive and often unsettling ways. Karl Mannheim, in *Ideology and Utopia*, describes a group phenomenon similar to the one confronting the Promise Keepers: "under what conditions may we say that the realm of experience of a group has changed so fundamentally that a discrepancy becomes apparent between the traditional mode of thought and the novel objects of experience."[18] For the Promise Keepers, the experienced discrepancy is the relationship between masculinity and femininity, what Judith Butler describes as the "sudden intrusion, the unanticipated agency, of a female "object" who inexplicably returns the glance, reverses the gaze, and contests the place and authority of the masculine position."[19] In other words, the dialectic between the two no longer provides a framework for understanding traditional gender.

Traditional (which is also hegemonic) gender, the masculine-feminine binary, is no longer an oppositional dialectic in need of an asymmetric other. An example would be a man's desire to be emotional; to be accepted as a man who cries and can embrace other men. Crying, in traditional gender ideology, is a feminine trait, a sign of softness and vulnerability, both of which are usually described as unmanly. But modern man wants to be accepted as one who is emotive, an identity traditionally denied the masculine male. The "new" performance framework would be male/androgyny and female/androgyny, with gender becoming blatantly descriptive and unontological. This expands both biological performances to Mannheim's "novel objects of experience" and destabilizes the "traditional mode of thought."

But male/androgyny is too amorphous, too formless, for a biblically rooted movement based on responsibility, accountability, and promise keeping. The Promise Keepers require something more structured and definable that can provide a foundation for a calculable identity. The foundation for an identity that can be held accountable is based on an alteration in the traditional symbolic order of male/masculine-female/feminine ideology; the Promise Keepers add a sign slide. Since femininity will not cooperate and provide the consistent other of masculinity, or since it shows that masculine autonomy is dubious,[20] the Promise Keepers elide femininity from the construction of masculinity. The Promise Keepers substitute the "known" masculine imago of Jesus Christ for the mysterious (unknown and/or unreliable) other of femininity. Since women no longer consistently reflect the other of masculinity, Christ becomes the touchstone. Instead of an asymmetrical reflection, masculinity is grounded in a symmetrical reflection of Christ. Femininity remains the mysterious other with no feminine divinity save the virgin mother. The dialectic is switched from the eternal feminine to Christ the eternal masculine. Woman no longer properly reflects; therefore, Christ becomes the reflexive ideal standard.

The imago of Christ as the eternal masculine is an ideologically violent and yet necessary aspect of the Promise Keepers gender ideology. It is violent in its dismissal of femininity; it is necessary in order to provide a foundation for masculinity. By altering the construction of the reflective other, by shifting the gaze, the Promise Keepers hope to solidify the content of the reflected form. Masculinity is posited as the reflected ideal of God's son; femininity is cast off as the unnecessary other without even engaging Simone de Beauvoir's question "why is woman the Other?" In this gender formation, women do not even get to be part of the questions asked.

The Promise Keepers book, *What Makes a Man?*, provides an example of the theoretical eliding of femininity from the construction of masculinity. In the chapter titled "The Promises You Make to Yourself," Smalley and Trent argue that there are "five marks of masculinity."[21] The five marks of biblical manhood are briefly defined and include independence, assertiveness, self-control, self-confidence, and stability. The definitions are all supplemented with anecdotal stories or testimonials concerning the topics and then supported with biblical evidence from the life of Jesus Christ. Smalley and Trent announce that "These key ingredients can be learned by a woman, but they set a man apart as a man."[22] They suggest to the men reading the book to keep in mind that these five marks come as a package; they define masculinity in any context, and these marks are "an ever-present nature in all men."[23]

The male "package" is naturalized; females can only learn (mimic) the package through a perversion of the natural order of things. When they do so, females go against their nature and succumb to social and cultural trends. This formulation is necessary for the Promise Keepers, because, if women can perform masculinity, and therefore be masculine, what would it mean for a man to be masculine?

As I discussed above, in order to save the concept of masculinity, the Promise Keepers move away from the traditional asymmetrical reflection of masculinity constructed as the other of femininity, a construction that reciprocates the other of an other. Instead, the Promise Keepers rely on a symmetrical reflection based on the masculine imago of Jesus Christ. This symmetrical reflection enables men to perform almost any characteristic and still remain within the parameters of biblical manhood as performed by Christ. Christ nurtured; men can nurture. Christ experienced fear; men can be afraid. Christ cried; men can cry. Christ doubted; men can have doubts. Christ was intimate with other men; men can be intimate with other men. Christ was a leader; men can be leaders.

This transhistorical and metaphysical masculine imago of Jesus Christ provides a constant and available psychological identification. As evangelical Christian men, the Promise Keepers accept a living imago that facilitates the operation of a masculine identity. But how is Jesus claimed as the true masculine imago and not a general human imago? In other words, what reference solidifies the Promise Keepers sole claim to Jesus Christ (the sacrificial *human* savior) as the ideal masculine imago; and how are women, by necessity, excluded from a natural identification with Jesus Christ?

## Nature

> Astronauts train their minds and fix a reference point; it is the only way they can live in their weightless environment. Christians do that too, all the time, in this "weightless" environment in which we live. For there are no fixed social values for us anymore, and if we function like the rest of society we will drift too. With no fixed position, no matter what we do, no matter what we try to push against, we will be useless.
>
> Roger Palms, "A Man's Fixed Reference"

> . . . that his nature is woven by effects in which we can find the structure of language, whose material he becomes, and that consequently there resounds in him, beyond anything ever conceived of by the psychology of ideas, the relation of speech.
>
> Jacques Lacan, *Feminine Sexuality*, "The Meaning of the Phallus"

An important tenet of the modern men's movement is that men can be more expressive toward other men. The male identity is decentered from traditional standards of manhood and can begin to forge atypical identities. This can be a moment of liberation and yet also of fear. If they are no longer constrained by patriarchy (no longer demanded by others to be the patriarch), then they can explore other identities. Yet this can cause an identity crisis. Freedom from predetermined roles is seductive, but the price of being seduced can be unlimited desire.

A significant part of the Promise Keepers message is that men can express emotions to and for other men. Women are not the only emotive beings, men can feel and express love and compassion in similar ways. Nonetheless, the Promise Keepers are very clear in stating that this is nothing more than a platonic form of love. This love can be expressed in the form of embraces, holding hands in prayer, and even in crying together. But it is always a nonsexual expression of affection. Homosexuality is a sin. It is not an option or an acceptable lifestyle. The Promise Keepers maintain an evangelical antihomosexuality position; the door to the closet remains open if the sin is repented.

Of the books and articles that the Promise Keepers have printed and endorsed on the topic of manhood, including Bill McCartney's *What Makes a Man* and Rodney Cooper's *Double Bind: Escaping the Contradictory Demands of Manhood,* the most interesting and controversial book is *The Masculine Journey: Understanding the Six Stages of Manhood,* by Robert Hicks. *The Masculine Journey* had been recommended and distributed by the Promise Keepers and they endorsed a study guide to facilitate the use of the book in small accountability groups.[24] The book was heavily criticized by other conservative Christians, with one study describing the effort as "replete with psychobabble, secular men's movement theory, forced exegesis, and gross theological error parading as biblical truth."[25] Since the book's publication in 1993, and the subsequent criticism it received for being unbiblical, the Promise Keepers have attempted to distance themselves from the book (they no longer distribute it at their conferences as they did in 1993), but they also have not repudiated or controverted it.[26]

*The Masculine Journey* provides a biblical understanding of what it means to be a man. Hicks divides manhood into six stages, which are illustrated through the use of the Hebrew words for man; they include the creational, phallic, warrior, wounded, mature, and sagely. According to Hicks, the creational stage reflects a man's "unique capabilities that are honorable and divine," the phallic stage his innate sexual focus, and the warrior stage his natural warring abilities exhibited on the athletic field, in the classroom, and in the business community.[27] The fourth stage described by Hicks is the wounded male, abused by external forces that include "absent fathers," "domineering mothers and teachers," layoffs, and divorce.[28] The fifth and sixth stages describe the man who is able to rule his own soul, through Christ, and the male who is a sage and mentor to others in his life.

According to Hicks, the phallic stage is the most troublesome for men in our culture. Hicks states that "Some men are very phallic-aware but have sort of fixated at the phallic stage of development. On the masculine journey they have stopped at Phallicville, found a sex-object, and built their whole life there."[29] The phallic stage differs from the other five in that it is seen as a stage that must be subdued rather than passed through or achieved. In other words, the male must learn to master his phallic stage in order to move on to the other stages of manhood.

The study guide that accompanies *The Masculine Journey* begins by asking the question "What does it mean to be a man?"[30] Throughout the book and study guide, being a man is described as a continual and dynamic process of growth and maturity. For Hicks and Dietrich Gruen, although being a man is not a static state, there is a "fixed point on the masculine journey" that grounds one's "identity as a man in something that will never change."[31] This fixed point is described by the Hebrew word *zakar*, more familiarly called the phallus, or the penis. At first this may appear insignificant to our understanding of the Promise Keepers; physiology has been used to demarcate the sexes in almost every historical culture and society. But this text does more than identify a male as a biological entity; it creates an identity based on that identification. Male becomes masculine. Sex becomes gender. The appearance of the phallus becomes an identity rather than a physiological identification. In other words, in this text, physiology does more than identify the sex of a human being, it also confers a natural and psychological identity.

This sliding from male into masculine, from physiology into psychology (and vice versa, from psychology to physiology), is important for an understanding of the Promise Keepers ideological practices because it highlights the attempt to produce masculinity as an unchanging and natural interpellation based on anatomy; an interpellation that will not fail (us). The individual is not hailed by another, but is instead hailed by his (and one assumes, her) anatomy. The interpellation becomes automatic, natural, and easily identifiable. This ideological practice signifies gender with clarity and simplicity, and constructs masculinity as biologically different than femininity. According to Hicks, the phallus also requires the male to maintain a special relationship with God based on his anatomy. Hicks states that:

> Possessing a penis places unique requirements upon men before God in how they are to worship Him. We are called to worship God as phallic kinds of guys, not as some sort of androgynous, neutered nonmales, or the feminized males so

popular in many feminist-enlightened churches. We are told by God to worship Him in accordance with what we are, phallic men.[32]

The phallus is transformed from a description of a physical reality to an expression of spirituality, and thus a state of being. A man's integrity becomes easily identifiable as a first order reflection of a basic reality with the signifier clearly exchanged for the signified. The phallus becomes the cause of masculinity rather than an effect of the systems of representation that order the social *bricolage*. The phallus becomes an alibi for action, a physiological and consistent stimulus because it signifies what is overdetermined.

But does the phallus signify masculinity? Postmodern and feminist theory argues that it only signifies male, and even that is debated. In these theories masculinity and femininity are often posited as overdetermined and nonessential characteristics. Masculinity would be something anyone could perform regardless of their genitalia. The Promise Keepers use of the phallus as an alibi for masculinity simplifies gender to something as obvious as physiology. As an ideological practice, the phallus-to-masculinity alibi becomes a powerful hypostasis that is easily comprehended by anyone willing to do so.

In the Promise Keepers formulation of masculinity, the phallus must signify masculinity or else he becomes speechless. He returns to the cave. He abdicates the leadership of the family. He becomes the people-pleaser and minion to popular opinion described by Smalley and Trent. The phallus = masculinity construction enables the Promise Keeper to speak by stabilizing that which is inherently unstable, the subject's relation to speech. In this economy, the phallus as signifier signifies the subject. The phallus functions as the "determinator" in the necessary division of the subject, *aphanisis* in the Lacanian sense of the term,[33] and posits (legitimates) an identity from which he can speak. Without the phallic guarantee, this essential division into the one from the Other, and the position ("stability") it provides, the subject is left undefined, pre-adjectival, and speechless. If the phallus does not signify masculinity in this economy, the male is left with the male/androgyny formation discussed earlier. But, as argued above, the male/androgyny position appears to the Promise Keepers to be too unstable, unbiblical, and feminine (culturalized) to provide a foundation for promise keeping. Androgyny is weightless, unpredictable, and uncalculable; not because androgyny is an inherently unstable identity, but rather because it refuses the minimalism of heterosexual gender ideology. It is unfoundational in the sense that it does not provide a consistent biological relation to speech. Promise keeping, by necessity, needs a consistent relation to speech. The subject has to be consistent, to speak from (with) consistency, in order to be accountable and responsible. The welding of penis to ontology, the signifier to a signified, marks and makes calculable one's relation to speech. In the *aphanisis*, the phallus is posited as that which will not fail (us).

It is important to reiterate what this "phallic kind of guy," according to Hicks, is not. He is not androgynous, neutered, or feminized. There is no perversion or concealment of who he is, because he is his anatomy. But to hypostatize masculinity in the image of the phallus is to render intelligible an overdetermined concept, all for the sake of providing a foundation for a male's identity. *The Masculine Journey*, endorsed and distributed by the Promise Keepers, conflates sex with gender in order to give men an anatomical (and biblical) foundation for their masculinity.

And yet, *The Masculine Journey* is less of an attempt to implement a reality than it is an effort to conceal the absence of a basic authenticity. *The Masculine Journey* attempts to ground masculinity in an unchanging natural referent in the absence of adequate and integral social references for masculinity. Jesus Christ provides the transhistorical reflexive other that is to be mirrored; the phallus provides a biological (historical) marker of the potential individuals who can naturally consummate the identification with the ideal. Women can learn the masculine way, but they can never naturally identify with the masculine imago. In today's "androgynous" and "feminized" reality, the Promise Keepers do not feel at home. The Promise Keepers find themselves in a world where masculinity lacks any real meaning. Since they no longer feel comfortable in the meaning of their masculinity, they adhere to an ideological practice that locates masculinity in an obvious and unchanging signifier, biology. Androgyny and femininity are negated in favor of a foundational and obvious masculinity. The panic over weightlessness is replaced by the naturalness of physiology. The question "What does it mean to be a man?" is answered by finding a natural haven for masculinity in an unreliable cultural order.

## Signature Moments

> Each one of us has a story to tell about how our life has unfolded. From the youngest little guy to the oldest man, there's a story that's threaded through our lives. I'd like to tell you some of my story – my testimony.
>
> Bill McCartney, "It's Time for Men to Take a Stand"

> I am now going to tell myself the story of my life.
>
> Friedrich Nietzsche, *Ecce Homo*

As stated above, gender identity is an obvious and yet elusive performance, always already bound to an ideological formation. With that in mind, perhaps masculinity can best be understood in the genre in which it is so readily performed, autobiographical or "signature moments." Signature moments provide narratives for an identity formation. They are the stories one tells oneself about oneself. Often, truth and falsehood become secondary reference points; signature moments are less concerned with accuracy and cohesion and tend to focus on therapeutics and performativity. Signature moments are simply those instances when individuals describe and come to terms with who they are.

One of the more interesting examples of this genre is Nietzsche's autobiography, *Ecce Homo: How one becomes what one is. Ecce Homo* is a textual example of a lifetime of signature moments. As a genre, the autobiography performs to itself. It narrates the (un)narrative, giving voice to that which can only be spoken in retrospect. For Nietzsche, the autobiographical genre was both a statement of fact and a fiction. *Ecce Homo* is Nietzsche's autobiography (in the form of a proper name) and also a parody, a comedic (ironic) production of that which never was. The literal meaning of *ecce homo* is "behold the man"; the symbolic significance is that *ecce homo* is also the title for a picture depicting Christ wearing the crown of thorns. In choosing the title of *Ecce Homo* for his autobiography, Nietzsche is welding the genre to a pre-sacrificial Jesus portrayed by his accusers as a false god. By doing so, Nietzsche is suggesting that to write one's autobiography is similar to honoring a false god and the pretensions of history. For Nietzsche, the autobiography was a modern crown of thorns, the false god of the modern self.

I will make a generalization: Everyone has his or her own story, his or her tape of signature moments. It is the tape one plays when someone is kind enough to ask and even generous enough to listen. When a Promise Keeper plays his tape, when he tells his story, he is in essence signing his name, his sig*nature*, saying 'behold the man'; he is always already an identity awaiting recognition. The sig*nature* is a man's sign that he has a story. It marks his nature, naturalizing and hypostatizing his being. Most people do not claim to be all the names of history, nor do many individuals perform more than one name. Individuals are either disciplined at an early age to form one identity, a proper name, or perhaps individuals find it the most comfortable and efficient way to maneuver through the world. In any case, a man's name, his sig*nature*, his crown of thorns, marks the beginning (and end) of his story.

The testimony is the most radical form of signature moment, and the one favored by the men leading the Promise Keepers. Testimony is a declaration and affirmation of the facts that have formed an individual's identity, experiences that make *one what one is.* Testimonials attest to the real; they reflect lived experiences, generally with a religious overtone. Testimonials are affirmations of the real, welding (marking) cause with effect. In a biblical sense, testimony is also the law of Moses inscribed on the tablets of stone, the word of God, the commandments, the truth. To give testimony is to provide evidence of that which was, and, by definition, of that which always will be.

The narratives and testimonials edited and produced by the Promise Keepers organization reflect both a hegemonic and nonhegemonic gender ideology, hegemonic referring to the traditional gender ideology, and nonhegemonic to the Christ-based masculinity. The Christ-based ideology, as mentioned earlier, substitutes the symmetric reflection of Jesus Christ for the asymmetric reflection of the eternal feminine. It is a nonhegemonic ideology because it is at present subsumed by the traditional reflective gender formation of male/masculine-female/feminine. Hegemony still reigns: asymmetric gender ideology is still the dominant way of understanding gender for men who identify themselves as Promise Keepers. The Christ-based symmetric ideology is usually only found in

Promise Keepers publications and given voice by men closely affiliated with the Promise Keepers, particularly the leadership.

There are at least three forms of signature moments that can be used to understand gender ideology and the men involved in Promise Keepers. These forms include the testimony, autobiography, and reverie. The first category, the testimony, is the most powerful form of gender construction, but also the least utilized. As suggested above, a testimony reflects a deep commitment to the truth, a testament to the way things are. They are not just localized explanations of the way one experiences the world; testimonies are local interventions of divine truth, a personal testament to God's truth. When Bob, a man I met at a Promise Keepers men's Bible study (see chapter one), told me his testimony regarding his experience of finding the Lord, it was a local intervention into his life by the Holy Spirit. It was, as he experienced it, God's truth. Typically, a testimony, when expressed to an audience, elicits responses of "Praise the Lord!" or "Yes Brother!" Often, a testimony concerning gender challenges the hegemonic ideology by replacing the eternal feminine with Christ.

An example of a testimonial gender formation is found in Rodney Cooper's book *Double Bind.* Cooper is the national director of educational services for the Promise Keepers. His book is an attempt to negotiate the contradictory demands placed on modern men. The following two excerpts from the book provide an example of the tension between the hegemonic gender ideology and the Christ-centered gender ideology offered by the Promise Keepers. The first testimony concerns an experience Cooper had while engaged in playground politics; the second positions Jesus Christ as the model of masculine authenticity.

### *Hegemonic Gender Construction*

> The age of five or six is key for a boy because that is when he begins to interact with other boys. To garner respect and have friends, he soon learns, he must not be like *girls.* I remember an incident in first grade that brought this fact home to me. While I was talking to one of my friends, another boy came up and began to put me down. I vividly recall him saying he did not like my jacket because it looked like something his sister would wear. I thought the best way to stay out of a fight was to ignore him. Wrong! He sucker punched me. While I was not looking, he hit me in the stomach as hard as he could. I immediately doubled over and found myself crying. The crying only lasted for a moment because all of my buddies were standing around to see how I would react. Instead, between huge gasps of air, I walked up to the guy who hit me and said, "It didn't hurt man - it didn't hurt," as I did everything I could to not break out crying. When the bell rang for recess to end, I acted like I needed to get something from behind a bush where I threw up and cried some more. I cried - but *they* (the guys) weren't going to see me cry. Even at six years of age it was important for me not to be seen as weak, needy, or in any way dependent because that would mean I was acting like a *girl.*[34]

*The Christ Model of Masculine Authenticity*

> A man caught in the double binds has learned to ignore his emotions. We saw, for instance, that in the Gender Bind, a man is afraid to stay in touch with any of his feminine traits because he doesn't want to be seen as wimpy by his friends. By suppressing these feelings he becomes alienated from an important part of himself. He may at times feel like crying, but won't let himself. If he even *feels* like crying he may think of himself as less of a man. After all, real men don't cry!
>
> Often, a man's conscious thoughts are disconnected from his emotions. And he can't seem to get them together. On the other hand, an authentic man is immediately conscious of his feelings because he knows who he is. He understands that his feminine feelings are part of being a man. When those emotions well up, he isn't afraid of them. He's in touch with them.
>
> In Gethsemane Jesus not only felt extreme grief, he expressed it to his disciples. He told them he was so depressed, that he was on the verge of death (Matt. 26:38). To understand why Jesus was in touch with his feelings we only need to go back a few hours in the story. Earlier in the night, while in the upper room, the words of John make it clear Jesus knew exactly who he was (John 13:3). He understood his relationship with his Father and his destiny. Jesus wasn't searching for his identity. *He knew!* That knowledge gave him the ability to connect with all of his emotions - even the negative ones.[35]

Cooper's playground testimonial and his call to masculine authenticity provide textual examples of the two theories of gender at work in the Promise Keepers. The playground testimonial is an example of hegemonic gender ideology as recalled by a middle-aged man. It is asymmetric: girls cry, boys do not. To be weak, needy, and in any way dependent is to be feminine. To be strong, in control, and independent is to be masculine. There is little remarkable in his testimony; it provides an example of generic hegemonic gender ideology.

But when Cooper discusses crying later in his book, crying is no longer a wholly female activity. Crying becomes a male activity, albeit a negative one. In this case the feminine traits are reflected in (by) Christ. Christ understood that "his feminine feelings are part of being a man." Gender is no longer an asymmetric reflection of masculinity in opposition to femininity; rather, Christ represents the symmetric other in a male's identity formation.

Another example of the Christ-like gender formation is found in the Promise Keepers book *What Makes a Man?* It is a discussion of one of the five marks of manhood; men's natural assertiveness. It is a testimony provided by John Trent about the natural assertiveness found in young boys but not in young girls and how assertiveness is naturally Christ-like.

> One mark of a man is the natural assertiveness that flows through his blood. Even toddlers reflect it.

> Instead of accepting the answer of ivory-tower radicals who expound theories of androgyny and blur the distinction between the sexes, spend some time talking to the mother of a boy and a girl. Their behavior patterns from the earliest ages show marked differences in natural aggression.
>
> My oldest brother, Joe, and his wife, Marnel, have two wonderful children – a girl and a boy. Mindy came along nearly four weeks premature, but with a fully developed peacefulness and warmth that has stayed with her for twelve years.
>
> With Mindy, Joe and Marnel never bothered to put away the decorative glass apple on the coffee table. One firm "no" the first time she picked up the crystal object and she obediently put it down and went on to other more acceptable playthings.
>
> Then Joseph came along. All boy, and all excited at his new found toddling skills, he headed for the coffee table and saw the pretty, crystal apple.
>
> "No, no," said Marnel, in her sweet, calm voice. "Put it down."
>
> *"Slam, slam, slam, slam!"* Joseph did put it down, smashing it down on the table as hard as he could to see if it would break (or at least to see how much noise it could make!).
>
> Within a week, everything breakable in the house had been evacuated from harm's way to avoid the might of this two-foot warrior of Diaper Storm.[36]

At this point in the testimony, the story reflects hegemonic gender ideology; young boys are more aggressive than young girls. This, by itself, is not remarkable. It is the next two paragraphs following this passage that exhibit the subtle yet important transition to a natural symmetric masculinity grounded in Christ. The testimony continues:

> It is in our deepest nature as men to push forward, to step out, to take charge, to fight for higher ground. The Shulammite woman saw this trait in Solomon and admired it as she said of his assertiveness, "Draw me after you, and let us run together."
>
> But while healthy assertiveness is an admirable trait, many men grow up taking two different directions that curve away from healthy assertiveness – and Christlikeness.[37]

Followed on the next page by:

> If you're missing this first mark of masculinity, then it's time to take a close look at your past and fill in the hole. But make sure that you don't fill it in by going to the opposite extreme when it comes to being assertive. We can have Christlike assertiveness without being domineering.[38]

Christ is the model of masculinity and it is not a masculinity relative to femininity. The truth is found in being Christ-like and not in traditional gender ideology. The signature of the testimony differs from the next example of autobiographical masculinity in the manner in which truth is guaranteed. The testimony deploys the model of Christ-likeness to guarantee masculinity; autobiographical masculinity submits truth to the manner in which gender is experienced. It relies on hegemonic gender ideology to organize and understand gender, stopping short of guaranteeing masculinity by calling on Christ.

The autobiography as gender narrative, as suggested above, is a weaker form of truth statement than the testimony; it is an individual's truth, his life experiences, without the metaphysical inclusion of God's truth. This type uses traditional hegemonic gender ideology to inform and construct masculinity. It is less than a testimony because it is a reflection on lived hegemonic gender experiences rather than parochial evidence of a greater truth.

Scot, a married and self-employed forty-three year old, provides an example of a Promise Keeper utilizing the autobiographical type of gender formation. I interviewed Scot at his office and I began with a question concerning the male's role in marriage. Scot responded by stating that men have been "unfaithful to the intent of the marriage vows." Scot then got up from his seat and left the room, returning in a few moments with a Bible. He then proceeded to read Scripture to me from Ephesians 5:22-28, on the relationship between the man and the woman in marriage.[39] Scot found this passage to be very clear and not open to interpretation. Marriage is a spiritual contract between a man and a woman and God. Men are subject to women and God, women are subject to men and God. For Scot, marriage is a sacrificial relationship - a male sacrifices his ego and desires to his wife and God; the woman reciprocates. Scot said that Promise Keepers promotes a selflessness toward the other, a giving up of the self to the other, a humbling of the self to the other. I acknowledged Scot's interpretation, and then asked him to go a little further in the mechanics of decision making. I asked Scot how selfless people, both respecting the other, could then come to a decision when they disagreed. He said that the husband, as the first among equals, has to make the decision. He supported this dynamic by referring to the Bible, actually pointing to it on the table. Men are not supposed to ignore or disregard their wives' opinions, but they are the decision makers. Scot was very comfortable with this reasoning.

Scot used the words "sacrifice" and "selfless" frequently while we were talking. He saw Promise Keepers as a way of reminding men of these themes and of making men accountable to their wives and children. He saw marriage as a relationship in which one attempts to minimize aggravation. He went on to tell me about certain "rules" he adheres to around the house; he never leaves dirty dishes in the sink, never leaves soiled clothes on the bathroom floor, puts things away in the kitchen, and so on. Scot is a detail person, priding himself on how he presents himself. He views marriage as taking care of the small things in life. He related the story to me that in six years of marriage his wife had only put gas in the car three times; once when he was in the hospital, once when he was out of town, and once when he forgot.

One of Scot's "fundamental beliefs" is that men and women are, by nature, different. Men are masculine and women are feminine. Women are more emotional, caring, sympathetic; men seem to be evil. On three occasions Scot referred to men (outside of a relationship with the Lord and the discipline of civil society) as hopelessly tempted. According to Scot, "men must be beaten into civility." Scot stated that "men would, if they could, run around on dope, drunk, and consorting with hookers, constantly." He only spoke about the evil/sinful ways of men, leaving it unclear if women are as capable of lust as men.

This led to a question concerning homosexuality. Scot had already mentioned homosexuality as a sin in the same context as rape and sexual abuse. He criticized homosexuality as an attack on God's children. He was willing to accept homosexuals as Christians, but only as Christians who were sinning. He accepted them as people, but could not tolerate their sinful lifestyle. He was making a distinction between the "act" and the person. The act is sinful; the person a child of God.[40]

Scot described feminists in the following manner: "Feminist women, and I hate to say this, are whiners." I had related to him that some of the criticism I had read about the Promise Keepers charged that the movement was attempting to "domesticate" women again by asking them to give up more and defer to men more often. He said that that point of view is based on fear, a feminist "conspiracy theory" that men are out to dominate. According to Scot, men are only out to lead according to biblical norms for marriage. He emphasized how far women had come since the 1950s and 1960s, that their progress to date has been nothing but phenomenal, but that all change takes time.

Direct questions regarding gender draw blank expressions from the men utilizing the autobiography to understand gender. They often appear surprised by the question. I attribute this reaction to their clear and concise understanding of gender; gender is something naturally found in each individual person. For Scot, gender is very simple; men are masculine and women are feminine. His gender signature moments are found in the details of his life, putting gas in his wife's car, picking up his soiled laundry, and helping out in the kitchen. These details, these simple everyday actions, are typical autobiographical moments that form one's gender identity. Scot thinks of himself as a man when he fills his wife's car with gas. He is proud of doing it. He enjoyed telling me this trivial fact. He feels masculine when he is taking care of this simple task for his wife. To Scot, if every man was as attentive to his spouse, many of society's problems could be resolved.

Scot's reliance on biological gender determination clarifies his world for him; women nurture by nature whereas men must "be beaten into civility." Scot typifies the type of man who discusses gender through his autobiography. Most of the Promise Keepers I have met view gender in this way. Gender remains something easily understood by these men. It is part of their nature and fundamental to the writing of their autobiography.

The third type of gender formation, the reverie, is completely autobiographical, but ambivalent and undecided about the role of gender. The men who use the reverie to understand gender are the second largest group among the Promise Keepers I have interviewed. Similarly to the previous categories, the reverie is also an individual's reflection on the way gender is experienced in contemporary culture, but it is not a statement of truth; rather, it is an abstracted musing on the importance of gender in one's life. The reverie is usually less than logical, yet it is thoughtful and reflective of gender experiences. But the importance of the reverie is the therapy it provides rather than the definitions it constructs. The reverie speaks in analogy and metaphor rather than truth and God.

John, a thirty-eight-year-old white male from a Midwestern city, provides an example of the type of Promise Keeper who uses the reverie to organize gender. John wants things in life, material things. But he does not consider himself a "materialist." That is how he describes women and, in particular, his exwife. She is a materialist because having things is how she feels good about herself. If she did not have the right car or did not have enough savings to buy frivolous things, then she was not happy. John claimed to believe in materialism, but to not be a materialist. He said that he has begun to ask God for material possessions, a new car or a new house. He said he does not think it will appear instantly, but that God will facilitate the process if he is deserving. John's feeling is that if he does not pray for it, God does not know he wants it. John also focused on the need to be practical, something his exwife never understood. He got a new sports car recently, but instead of getting the two seater like he usually does, he decided instead to get a sports car with four seats. He also switched from Mitsubishi to Chrysler, because for practically the same car, Chrysler was a couple of thousand dollars cheaper.

John was previously married to Sara for 12 years and has two children, Dave who is ten and Michalah who is six. John identifies himself as an "entrepreneur," a selfmade man. But he adds that he is still in the process of "making it" and that this process was one of the problems that led to his divorce from Sara. He would work, but "never made enough to satisfy her." He has bounced from business to business, always willing to try new opportunities. Some of these are more successful than others, but more often than not, it seems that his endeavors did not match his, or his exwife's, expectations. John is a dreamer; he is confident that he is going to make it big. On several occasions he would list off salaries of "$30,000, $40,000, $50,000, $60,000," and then he would state "but I want $150,000."

John really is not over his divorce yet. In discussing almost every topic, he would find a way of bringing his marriage to Sara into the conversation. Sometimes it was appropriate, as when we were discussing family, marriage, and relationships. But even when we were talking about Jesus, Promise Keepers, or even other men in the church, somehow Sara would end up being discussed. It was during the divorce and immediately afterwards that John got involved with Promise Keepers.

John is ambivalent toward gender, particularly as it relates to issues of sexuality. It was difficult for him to give me his opinion on homosexuality. This was particularly interesting given the willingness of the other types of Promise Keepers to discuss homosexuality. The men expressing themselves through testimony and autobiography do not hesitate. They have clear and readily available ideological positions regarding homosexuality. The men utilizing the reverie, however, only voice their opinion after two or three attempts to engage them in the discussion.

John stated that he has some gay and lesbian friends and has worked with openly homosexual friends, but he was still somewhat uncomfortable discussing the subject. After some further prompting, he made an analogy to a football team. According to John, a football team needs all kinds of players. These players have to be different sizes, have different abilities, and provide different talents. If they all were the same, the team would not function very well. But with diversity, with everyone contributing in the best way they can, the team has a better chance of success.

John went on to explain that all the members of the team may cooperate for the good of the team, but that they do not always socialize together. He then jumped to a basketball analogy, pointing out that he likes Purdue basketball fans, works with them, and even has some of them as friends, but that he prefers to root for Indiana. He concluded by saying that he would not want to be around Purdue fans all the time; he does not like to watch a ball game with them.

John, as is typical of many Promise Keepers, has thought about gender and has decided that it is sometimes confusing. John thinks there are differences between men and women, but he struggles with any clear definition of what those differences may be. John's musings on materialism are an attempt to find some logical difference. His conclusion is reflective of what often happens in the reverie type of gender formation, a convoluted deliberation on difference. John wants material things, but he does not see himself as a materialist; his exwife is a materialist. John wants a sports car *and* he wants to be practical. John wants to think of himself as a practical man, a lesson he learned from his father, and also the opposite of how he constructs his exwife.

The reverie gender formation is typified by men struggling to understand their gender. Gender is something that appears to provide them an identity, but the identity is more or less undecided. It is an identity with little truth value. This is their main difference from the more decided Promise Keepers, who are comfortable utilizing the testimony or autobiography formation. The reverie is not a truth statement. At best, the reverie is an investigation of gender with an understanding that one may be wrong. The men discussing gender through reveries are unsure of the truthfulness of their claims, but they attempt to order the disorder. John's use of sports analogies is a familiar technique to all the men talking about gender through reveries. The analogy distances their discussion of gender from any truth statement, and yet it approximates an understanding and affirmation from a likeminded individual.

## Concluding Thought

In discussing the Promise Keepers and the concept of gender, one finds a reliance on traditional or hegemonic gender ideology constructed as male/masculine-female/feminine. This construction still has mass appeal, as suggested by the growth and success of Promise Keepers events, and provides men with an easily understood and comfortable identity formulation. But there is also another gender message within the Promise Keepers discourse, one that replaces the traditional role of reflective femininity with Christ the masculine imago. This formulation is remarkable since masculinity and males are presented as being in a natural symmetric relationship with Jesus Christ, the son of God. There is no corresponding "daughter" of God in Christian theology. The role of femininity becomes unstable in this construction of gender, neither bound to masculinity nor having a metaphysical symmetric other. Masculinity is allowed a symmetrical relationship with the son of God, and femininity is presented as a gender position that is less than divine.

A symbolic order that attempts to clarify by distilling an essential foundation for gender is nothing new. What is interesting about the Promise Keepers is their reliance on traditional gender ideology combined with an attempt to provide a metaphysical symmetric foundation for masculinity. Perhaps Baudrillard offers a timely counsel on the peril of such constructions:

> If we take to dreaming once more – particularly today – of a world where signs are certain, of a strong 'symbolic order', let's be under no illusions. For this order has existed, and it was a brutal hierarchy, since the sign's transparency is indissociably also its cruelty.[41]

## Notes

1. Promise Keepers letter to conference attendees 1996.

2. Ibid.

3. The letter from Paul to Timothy contains advice on how to order and structure a congregation. The following are some of the accompanying citations. "11th A woman should learn in quietness and full submission. 12th I do not permit a woman to teach or to have authority over a man; she must be silent. 13th For Adam was formed first, then Eve. 14th And Adam was not the one deceived; it was the woman who was deceived and became a sinner." (NIV: Zondervan, 1996).

4. This perspective is also expressed by Robert Hicks, "Why Men Feel So Out of Place at Church," in *What Makes a Man?*, ed. Stephen Griffith (Colorado Springs: NavPress, 1992), 154-156. Hicks writes that the church is "essentially an institution that appeals more to women than to men" and that he is "amused over the current debate about ordaining women . . . as if women have never had any power in the church." (154)

On the following page Hicks concludes that "We must recapture the church for men, defeminize it, and make our appeals to men where it will cost them something more than their money or their time. Christ wants their lives." (155)

5. Michael S. Kimmel, *Manhood in America: A Cultural History* (New York: The Free Press, 1996), 179.

6. Ibid., 179. See also Michael A. Messner, *Politics of Masculinities: Men in Movements* (Thousand Oaks, CA: Sage Publications, 1997), 24-35.

7. Ibid., 180.

8. See Charles Stanley, "The Sensitive Man and Romance," in *What Makes a Man?*, ed. Stephen Griffith (Colorado Springs: NavPress, 1992), 82; E. Glenn Wagner, with Dietrich Gruen, *Strategies For A Successful Marriage: A Study Guide For Men* (Colorado Springs: NavPress, 1994), 12; Gregg Lewis, *The Power of a Promise Kept: Life Stories by Gregg Lewis* (Colorado Springs: Focus on the Family Publishing, 1995), 149-162; Rodney L. Cooper, *Double Bind: Escaping the Contradictory Demands of Manhood* (Grand Rapids, MI: Zondervan Publishing House, 1996), 127-141. An example is the following quote from Larry Crabb "Masculinity," in *What Makes a Man?*, ed. by Stephen Griffith (Colorado Springs: NavPress, 1992): "It is the demonstrated and eager sensitivity to another's need that feels masculine to both partners when a husband rubs his wife's sore neck" (48).

9. Gary Smalley and John Trent, "The Promises You Make to Your Wife," in *What Makes a Man?*, ed. by Stephen Griffith (Colorado Springs: NavPress, 1992), 61.

10. Ibid., 62.

11. The man's inability to lead the family is described by Dr. Tony Evans, a Promise Keepers conference speaker and author, as the primary cause of the national crisis in today's family. See Tony Evans, "Spiritual Purity," in *Seven Promises of a Promise Keeper*, ed. Al Janssen (Colorado Springs: Focus on the Family Publishing, 1994), 73-81:

> For years, sociologists have argued over the causes of the problem (i.e., the decline of the American family). Politicians have thrown billions of dollars into our cities, hoping that would solve the riddle. Others have stood by, scratching their heads, wondering where society went wrong. In the meantime, the negative statistics soar and the lives of countless children are irreparably damaged. I am convinced that the primary cause of this national crisis is the feminization of the American male. When I say *feminization*, I am not talking about sexual preference. I'm trying to describe a misunderstanding of manhood that has produced a nation of "sissified" men who abdicate their role as spiritually pure leaders, thus forcing women to fill the vacuum. (73)

12. It is interesting to note that this "particularly feminine ailment" is also cited as an area of concern in the mythopoetic movement. Robert Bly, *Iron John: A Book About Men* (Reading, MA: Addison-Wesley Publishing, 1990), states the following:

> In the seventies I began to see all over the country a phenomenon that we might call the "soft male." Sometimes even today when I look out at an audience, perhaps half the young males are what I'd call soft. They're lovely, valuable people – I like them - they're not interested in harming the earth or starting wars. There's a gentle attitude toward life in their whole being and style of living. (2-3)

> The "soft" male was able to say, "I can feel your pain, and I consider your life as important as mine, and I will take care of you and comfort you." But he could not say what he wanted, and stick by it. Resolve of that kind was a different matter. (4)
>
> The journey many American men have taken into softness, or receptivity, or "development of the feminine side," has been an immensely valuable journey, but more travel lies ahead. No stage is the final stop. (4)

13. See also Robert Hicks, "Why Beer Commercials Make Some Men Feel So Good," in *What Makes a Man?*, ed. Stephen Griffith (Colorado Springs: NavPress, 1992); Hicks states that "The close, nonsexual presence of other men will affirm our manhood more than anything else. Through these encounters, we validate our experiences as men, lose our deep-seated dependence on women, and find the same-gender counterpart we need who truly understands what it is like to be a man." (137) E. Glenn Wagner, "Strong Mentoring Relationships," in *Seven Promises of a Promise Keeper,* ed. Al Janssen (Colorado Springs: Focus on the Family Publishing, 1994), adds the same concern in a section titled 'The So-called New Man': "Can a "real man" enjoy a deep and meaningful, nonsexual relationship with another man? The answer is yes." (58)

14. William Bell Riley, *Wives of the Bible: A Cross-Section of Femininity* (Grand Rapids, MI: Zondervan, 1938), 123.

15. Michael Schwalbe, *Unlocking the Iron Cage: The Men's Movement, Gender Politics, and American Culture* (New York: Oxford University Press, 1996), 37-46; see also Messner, *Politics of Masculinities*, 20-21.

16. Bly, *Iron John*, 5.

17. Judith Butler, *Gender Trouble: Feminism and the Subversion of Identity* (New York: Routledge, 1990), vii-xi; Joan W. Scott, "Experience," in *Feminists Theorize The Political*, ed. Judith Butler and Joan W. Scott (New York: Routledge, 1992), 35.

18. Karl Mannheim, *Ideology and Utopia: An Introduction to the Sociology of Knowledge*, trans. Louis Wirth and Edward Shils (New York: A Harvest Book, 1985), 100-101. (Original work published 1936.)

19. Butler, *Gender Trouble*, vii.

20. Ibid., vii-viii.

21. Gary Smalley and John Trent, "The Promises You Make to Yourself," in *What Makes a Man?,* ed. Stephen Griffith (Colorado Springs: NavPress, 1992), 39.

22. Ibid., 39.

23. Ibid., 39.

24. Both book covers, Hicks' text and the study guide, bear the Promise Keepers logo.

25. David Hagopian and Douglas Wilson, *Beyond Promises: A Biblical Challenge to Promise Keepers* (Moscow, ID: Canon Press, 1996), 93. See also David W. Cloud, "Beware of Promise Keepers," *O Timothy Magazine,* 11, no. 6 (Reprint, 1994), 2; Phil Arms, *Promise Keepers: Another Trojan Horse* (Houston, TX: Shiloh Publishers, 1997), 211-215; Ami Neiberger, "Promise Keepers: Seven Reasons to Watch Out," *Freedom Writer* (Institute for First Amendment Studies, September 1996), 4-5.

26. Letter from Promise Keepers, May 21, 1997, providing their official statement concerning *The Masculine Journey*. The following paragraphs are the pertinent parts of the letter:

> Several passages in *The Masculine Journey* by Robert Hicks (1993, NavPress) could be understood in more than one way. Some of the content of the book has unfortunately lent itself to a wide range of interpretations and responses involving theological issues which Promise Keepers does not feel called to resolve. These are controversies which neither Promise Keepers nor the author could have foreseen, and which have proven to be a distraction from the focus of our ministry. Therefore, Promise Keepers has discontinued marketing and distributing *The Masculine Journey.*
>
> At the same time, we believe Mr. Hicks' core theology is consistent with orthodox evangelical Christianity, and that *The Masculine Journey* was a forthright attempt on his part to deal with male issues from a biblical context.

27. Robert Hicks and Dietrich Gruen, *The Masculine Journey: A Promise Keepers Study Guide* (Colorado Springs: NavPress, 1993), 9.

28. Ibid., 9-10.

29. Robert Hicks, *The Masculine Journey: The Six Stages of Manhood* (Colorado Springs: NavPress, 1993), 24.

30. Hicks and Gruen, *The Masculine Journey: A Promise Keepers Study Guide*, 5.

31. Ibid., 28.

32. Hicks, *The Masculine Journey*, 51. For a similar discussion of 'the androgynous man,' see Gorsuch, *BROTHERS!*, 102.

33. Lacan, *Feminine Sexuality*, 16.

34. Rodney L. Cooper, *Double Bind: Escaping the Contradictory Demands of Manhood* (Grand Rapids, MI: Zondervan Publishing House, 1996), 38. All italics in original. The headings "Hegemonic Gender Construction" and "The Christ Model of Masculine Authenticity" are my own and not taken from Cooper's book.

35. Ibid., 158.

36. Gary Smalley and John Trent, "The Promises You Make to Yourself," in *What Makes a Man?*, ed. Stephen Griffith (Colorado Springs: NavPress, 1992), 40.

37. Ibid., 40.

38. Ibid., 41.

39. Ephesians 5:22-28.

> [22]Wives, submit to your husbands as to the Lord. [23]For the husband is the head of the wife as Christ is the head of the church, his body, of which he is the Savior. [24]Now as the church submits to Christ, so also wives should submit to their husbands in everything.
>
> [25]Husbands, love your wives, just as Christ loved the church and gave himself up for her [26]to make her holy, cleansing her by the washing with water through the word, [27]and to present her to himself as a radiant church, without stain or wrinkle or any other blemish, but holy and blameless. [28]In this same way, husbands ought to love their wives as their own bodies. He who loves his wife loves himself.

40. This is a common way that Promise Keepers deal with the question of homosexuality. It is a phrase that has wide spread use among individual Promise Keepers as well as the printed materials from the national office.

41. Jean Baudrillard, *Symbolic Exchange and Death*, trans. Iain Hamilton Gain (Thousand Oaks, CA: Sage Publications, 1995), 50.

# Chapter Five

---

## Stand in the Gap: A Prophet from Babylon

The bus was about an hour from RFK stadium, our designated parking area, and Steve, the organizer of the trip, led the 46 men in prayer. He then asked if any of the men wanted to come forward and share their thoughts and expectations for the day ahead, the Promise Keepers assembly in Washington, D.C. Jim, the trip's emotional sparkplug, took the bus microphone and told the men "It's time to get pumped up! It's time to 'stand in the gap'!"

Jim's exhortation "to get pumped up" prompted several men to come forward and to share their thoughts. The first man to come forward said that "this day would surely please the Lord – the sight of literally thousands of buses streaming toward the capital must be making God smile." The next speaker, a white man with gray hair, said that this assembly was exactly what "this country needs." A black man took the microphone, and in a somber voice filled with emotion, quietly talked about the spirit of love pervading the bus. He said that this was a day he would always remember.

He was followed by the man everyone on the bus affectionately called "Hippie." Hippie had long hair, a full beard, and wore a shirt that had four alien looking figures on the front with the slogan "Lust patrol." The back of his black shirt was emblazoned in white with the message "The Only Kind of Safe Sex is the Kind Practiced with Your Marriage Partner." Hippie, enthusiastically addressing the men on the bus, said that "We are part of a great revival – part of this enormous gathering – part of Christ's power." Four other men approached the microphone and gave brief testimonies. Some of the men talked about the problems confronting families and men; others wanted to pray for the nation and for marriages. After this, Hippie led the men in singing "Blessed be the name of the Lord."

After the song, Steve asked the men to "rid themselves of unconfessed sin." He said the sacred assembly was about repentance of sin and that the men should take a few moments to reflect on their sins. He told the men that they were part of "an army" and that they had to make sure there was "no unconfessed sin in the camp." Steve then called for a few minutes of private reflection before he led the men in prayer, asking the Lord to bless the sacred assembly. He closed by noting that "the important decisions are not made in DC, but are made in the hearts of Americans everyday of the week."

Steve then introduced Bob, who led the men in a communion service, using Pepperidge Farms' 'fishes' as wafers washed down with cups of Welch's grape juice.

Stand in the Gap: A Sacred Assembly of Men was the official theme of the Promise Keepers gathering in Washington, D.C., on October 4, 1997. The first part of the thematic program was developed from Ezekiel 22:30, where God speaks to Ezekiel about the sins of Jerusalem: "I looked for a man among them who would build up the wall and *stand* before me *in the gap* on behalf of the land so I would not have to destroy it, but I found none" (my italics).

The reference to the book of Ezekiel is indicative of Promise Keepers perceived need for a great awakening and modern Christian revival. Ezekiel was God's prophet to his people while they were enslaved in Babylon. Specifically, the 22nd chapter of Ezekiel is God's message to Ezekiel about the unrepented sins of his people. In verses 3-14, God accuses the people of Jerusalem of worshiping idols, committing lewd acts, of dishonoring women when they are ceremonially unclean, of incest, and murder. In verse 15 God warns the people that "I will put an end to your uncleanness." Verses 17-22 detail how God will bring his wrath to bear on his people. Verses 23-29 discuss the failures of the nation's priests: "they do not distinguish between the holy and the common," nor the clean from the unclean.[1]

Verse 30, the one used by the Promise Keepers, tells of God's desire to find a man who will stand against such treachery, but God cannot find one. The 22nd chapter closes with these words from verse 31: "So I will pour out my wrath on them and consume them with my fiery anger, bringing down on their own heads all they have done, declares the Sovereign Lord."

The Promise Keepers are signifier savvy; they package a critique of licentious behavior and unrepented sin in a challenge to men to stand with God rather than against Him. In Ezekiel, God's people have walked away from a relationship with Him. Using Ezekiel's critique of Babylon as a biblical starting point, 'Stand in the Gap' was a call for men to stand with God rather than siding with the idol worshippers and false images of a modern day Babylon. It was a call for men to stand with God before it is too late. The Ezekiel metaphorical paradigm is clear: Babylon rules today, but God is looking for a few good men to stand with Him and save the nation from destruction.

The second part of the Promise Keepers thematic program, the call for "A Sacred Assembly of Men," was based on the Old Testament record of sacred assemblies and binds one's individual relationship with God to the greater community. According to the Promise Keepers, "the Old Testament records twelve instances when Israel was called by God to gather for one or more days of prayer, fasting, confession, and repentance of sin because the nation had wandered away spiritually and morally."[2] The theme of community was based on 2 Chronicles 15 7:14.[3] This verse depicts the word of the Lord spoken to Solomon (I have included verses 12-13 for context):

> 12the Lord appeared to him at night and said: "I have heard your prayer and have chosen this place for myself as a temple for sacrifices.
>
> 13"When I shut up the heavens so that there is no rain, or command locusts to devour the land or send a plague among my people, 14if my people, who are called by my name, will humble themselves and pray and seek my face and turn from wicked ways, then will I hear from heaven and will forgive their sin and will heal their land.

The two parts of the program emphasize the individual's role within the community. Similar to the chapter on social capital and the discussion of communitarian theory in previous chapters of this writing, the Promise Keepers D.C. rally combined the functionalism of the individual ("I looked for a man among them who would build up the wall and stand before me in the gap") with the necessity and power of the community (a sacred assembly of men).

The men on the bus felt they were part of something special. As we traveled across Indiana, Ohio, and Pennsylvania, the stream of buses and cars carrying Promise Keepers grew ever more obvious and impressive. By the time we stopped on the morning of October 4 in Breezewood, PA, the scene reminded me of one I had witnessed many times before – a predawn army mobilization exercise, complete with units of men organized (the buses usually had individual church identifications, such as "Willow Creek for SITG!") and armed, except this army carried Bibles instead of guns.

## NOW Press Conference

> Racist, Sexist, Antigay
> Born Again Bigots Go Away!
> Chant at NOW Promise Keepers Protest

The National Organization for Women (NOW) protest at the Promise Keepers assembly was located three blocks from the main stage on a grassy triangle bounded by 1st Street and Constitution and Louisiana Avenue. The triangle was surrounded by ten foot tall posters with inflammatory quotes from Promise Keepers leaders:

> Abortion has become "a second Civil War." Bill McCartney, *Denver Post*, February 11, 1992.
>
> "There is no way the group can restrict itself when it comes to public policy. We are producing leaders in this organization. They will enter the public sphere." Raleigh Washington, *Dallas Observer*, November 14, 1996.
>
> "The demise of our community and culture is the fault of sissified men who have been overly influenced by women." Tony Evans, *The Progressive*, August 1996.
>
> "We will not compromise. Whenever the truth is at risk, in the schools or legislature, we are going to contend for it. We will win." Bill McCartney, *Freedom Writer*, September 1996.

As men walked by the protest on their way to the PK rally, protestors lined the sidewalk chanting slogans and waving NOW placards with the slogan "Fight the Radical Right – NOW." The protestors also carried homemade signs asking the Promise Keepers to support women's equality and to denounce institutional racism. One sign that drew expressions of disgust from many men passing by proclaimed that "Real Men Don't Need God."

The protestors were mostly college age women and men with a few older supporters. Conspicuously absent was support from middle-aged women. Promise Keepers draws support from across the age spectrum, but is predominantly a movement of middle-aged men. For example, the ages of the men gathered on the mall ranged from young boys to elderly grandfathers, but most were men in their 30s and 40s. The NOW protest was dominated by young adults.[4]

The protest culminated in a press conference by NOW that was also supported by several other prowomen and equality groups. Speakers included NOW President Patricia Ireland, Eleanor Smeal from Feminist Majority, Al Ross from the Center for Democracy Studies, Pamela Coukas from the National Coalition Against Domestic Violence, and Mandy Carter from Equal Partners in Faith.

As the press conference started, a man standing next to me wearing a shirt with the "PK: Men of Integrity" embroidered on the chest asked in a soft voice, why NOW and the other protestors referred to the Promise Keepers as 'racist'? Before I could respond, a woman standing in front of us wearing a NOW sticker whirled around and caustically stated that "If you want to talk, go somewhere else." I responded that I was just trying to address the man's question and that I was not a Promise Keeper. This seemed to satisfy her concerns since she turned around, received a hug from a supporter, and let us return to our conversation without further interruption.

The man, Wayne Purcell, who flew to the assembly with 20 men from California, was confused by the disparaging word 'racist' associated with the Promise Keepers movement. I told him that NOW portrays PK as racist because they do not fight racism in the same manner as NOW. As part of NOW's Promise Keepers Mobilization Project on their Homepage, one finds a list of "Myths and Facts about the Promise Keepers." The myth, according to NOW, is that "PK advocates an end to racism." The fact, according to NOW, is that;

> While the Promise Keepers claim to want to end racism, they are only giving lip service. They are not working to end the institutional racism in society today, but are working on programs of "racial reconciliation" through personal relationships.[5]

NOW's criticism of racial reconciliation as "only giving lip service" in the fight against racism is misleading and unnecessarily political. It also elides the lived experiences of literally thousands of men, of all races, who claim racial progress through their involvement in Promise Keepers. NOW cannot accept PK as a spiritual movement, thus their insistence (dogma?) that one must fight racism NOW's way. Since PK "only" supports racial reconciliation (which asks men to commit to breaking down racial barriers, to repent the sin of racism, and to form a relationship with a man of another race) they are not fighting racism in the acceptable radical-liberal manner. In NOW's perspective, Promise Keepers are only giving lip service to fighting racism when they publish a 200-page workbook on overcoming racial barriers;[6] or when they dedicate a cover story in *New Man* magazine supporting interracial marriages and decrying the hatred and bigotry that interracial couples must endure.[7] Fighting racism from a biblical perspective appears to make PK 'racist.'[8]

At the press conference, Patricia Ireland, President of NOW, asked the Promise Keepers to agree to a New Promise, to respect women's equality. The call for an addendum promise is based on NOW's concerns regarding Ephesians 5:22, which states "Wives, submit to your husbands as to the Lord." The NOW 'Myth and Fact' sheet engages the "myth" that the Promise Keepers are good for women by stating that "Promise Keepers openly call for wives to submit to their husbands."[9]

The official publications of the Promise Keepers do not attempt to interpret Ephesians 5:22. They do discuss a Christian perspective on marriage and a husband's and wife's role within the institution, but the discussion never focuses on submission. Promise Keepers literature on marriage is based on the ideals of partnership, communication skills, and relationship building. They are often criticized by other conservatives for incorporating psychology into a biblical understanding of marriage. E. Glenn Wagner's *Strategies for a Successful Marriage*, the Promise Keepers primary study guide for men on marriage, has chapters titled "Men Don't Ask Directions," "Communication Within Marriage," and "Whatever Happened to Romance and Fun?" Some of the marriage advice given by Wagner includes the following:

> The macho idea that men must make all the decisions, or have the final say, is not what marriage is about. Marriage is about a vibrant partnership, two coming together as one – and those two submerging their wills and living for the glory of God.[10]

Of all the texts from the Promise Keepers on marriage, the most sensational call for male leadership is Tony Evans' oftquoted demand for men to take back the leadership of the marriage: "I am not suggesting you *ask* for your role back, I'm urging you to *take it back*."[11] But Evans is not discussing submission (although it seems to be inferred), but rather spiritual leadership. It is important to note, that in the same essay where he urges men to take back the leadership of the family, Evans models the "spiritually pure man" after Job, the great innocent sufferer. Job, the spiritually pure man, is described as a God-fearing man with the following characteristics: a divine continuity with the past, committed to raising children, earns respect, a man of mercy, a person of justice and stability, and a man of wisdom.[12]

On the question of Christian submission, Promise Keepers at the local level usually have formed an opinion. Men I have interviewed will openly discuss what it means for the woman to submit to her husband as to the Lord (Ephesians 5:22) and the male's role of servanthood as leadership within the family. The men usually point to the "as to the Lord" part of the verse, highlighting the importance of submission to the Lord for both parties in the marriage. Some Promise Keepers emphasize the importance of male leadership through service to the family, while others have noted the small number of times a man is placed in a position where he has to make a decision. Mike, a member of the bus entourage, described the advice given to him by a mentor in his church concerning the submission of wives and male leadership within the family. The elder told Mike that "If you can't persuade your wife to your point of view, it may be God's way of telling you it's a bad idea."

The ideal of Christian submission within a marriage is a highly charged and important, although often confusing, issue. It addresses fundamental values and concerns of leadership and equality within the family. There is also another issue, and one that I believe to be of equal importance for understanding the Promise Keepers, concerning the role of women in a specific leadership position: the ordination of women. I was surprised that the issue was not addressed by NOW at the PK press conference. This is a major contemporary political and theological issue since 50 percent of seminary students are women.

The Promise Keepers do not address the issue directly in their publications, but their position is evident through their actions, if not their words. Female pastors are conspicuously absent from Promise Keepers clergy events. Women were not invited nor encouraged to attend the PK Atlanta Clergy conference held in 1996. They were also not invited to participate in the pastors and church leaders conferences (see Chapter Four) held prior to stadium events in both 1996 and 1997.

The Promise Keepers I have interviewed often refer to 1 Timothy 2:11-15 concerning the ordination of women. The order of things, or what is often referred to as the "plumb line," proscribes women from positions of leadership. The passage discusses Paul's guidance to Timothy in leading churches:

> [11]A woman should learn in quietness and full submission. [12]I do not permit a woman to teach or to have authority over a man; she must be silent. [13]For Adam was formed first, then Eve. [14]And Adam was not the one deceived; it was the woman who was deceived and became a sinner. [15]But women will be saved through childbearing – if they continue in faith, love and holiness with propriety.

The ordination of women as church leaders is a potentially divisive issue between Promise Keepers and mainstream denominations. Such doctrinal conflict could foment discontent with Promise Keepers from denominational leaders, which could combine with calls for equality profeminist groups. Since the Promise Keepers have scheduled nine one-day clergy conferences in the spring of 1998 to foster a partnership between pastors and their men's ministries, it seems that this question will begin to receive more attention as a potentially theological and political issue among both denominational leaders and groups such as NOW.

One might ask why Promise Keepers should include female clergy in its deliberations since it is a men's movement? The question involves the issue of leadership within the church. The pastor, as the leader of the congregation, is responsible for all aspects of ministry within the church. If female clergy are not involved in or actively excluded from directing the men's ministry within their own congregation, the effect would be to undermine the pastor's ability to minister God's word, the opposite effect of PK stated mission.

If the absence of female pastors from the 1998 clergy conferences potentially undermines how a Promise Keeper honors his pastor (Promise Five), it also works against the overall purpose of the clergy conferences. Promise Keepers stated intention is to encourage clergy to meet to discuss local issues of concern and then return to their men's ministry to inform the members of the problems confronting the community. It would appear that the sex of the pastor would be insignificant in disseminating information to the men in the congregation. It is not as if the female clergy would have to lead a discussion of the men's group concerning the evils of lust and pornography, issues PK have told me they would not be comfortable discussing with a female pastor. Rather, in gathering, organizing, and disseminating information, the pastor is functioning as the leader of the congregation while also making men aware of the needs of the community.

## The Mall

I arrived on the mall at about ten in the morning, two hours before the scheduled start of the assembly. The grassy areas between the Capitol Building and the Washington Monument were already filled to capacity, with the crowd spilling over onto the side streets and the hillside beyond the monument. I left the three men from my bus group, who had rode the Metro train with me, and began to walk around the mall.

One of the first objects to catch my attention were the white canvassed teepees placed on the mall. They were approximately 15 feet tall and erected to the left and right of each Jumbotron. Each teepee had a sign that described its function i.e., "Prayer Teepee." The teepees reminded me of something I had read concerning the assembly. The Promise Keepers were going to have Native Americans open the sacred gathering with a traditional Native American greeting, which they did at 12:00.

The significance of having Native Americans open the assembly was addressed before the gathering by Dale Schlafer, Promise Keepers vice president of Revival and Awakening, on their Homepage. Schlafer said that Native Americans would be hosting the event "because we want to show that we are sorry for what transpired on their land, and that as brothers in Christ, we want them to take the lead in this event."[13] Schlafer also discussed the Scriptural evidence for having musical instruments announce the beginning of sacred assemblies: "In the Old Testament, the shofar (a ram's-horn trumpet) was blown prior to battles to signify the army of God" (ibid.). He went on to say that the consecrating trumpet call would announce the "arrival of royalty, the Lord of lords and King of kings."[14]

During the assembly, the bustle of men on the mall was more racially diverse than other Promise Keepers events have been. Also, as the day went on, there were many women in the crowd. Earlier in the day, women were helping Promise Keepers with such supportive tasks as the distribution of Bibles and crowd control. But as the afternoon drifted on, the women became part of the assembly, participating through prayer and moments of reflection (although I did not witness any women participating with men in small prayer groups).

Many of the women at the assembly were curiosity seekers. Jim, the entourages "convicted" (someone with committed faith in the Lord) motivator, told me about two women he met at the Lincoln Memorial. In the course of conversation, the women began asking him questions about the Promise Keepers, the crowd on the mall, and the list of speakers. Jim suggested that the women go to the mall and see the assembly for themselves. The women were surprised at the invitation since they were under the impression that the assembly was only for men. Jim told the women that today was a special day, a day for anyone who believed in Christ or who wanted to learn more about Christianity.

Jim's message to the women at the Lincoln Memorial parallels one delivered by the Promise Keepers as part of the program. Early in the afternoon, Randy Phillips, the President of Promise Keepers, told the assembly (and those watching on television), that the men gathered on the mall were "not there to exalt their gender but to exalt our savior, who is God." He also said that "no woman should feel threatened by Promise Keepers, but that they should have hope that they may be conformed to live like Jesus."

As I wandered the mall I saw what has become the typical Promise Keepers atmosphere – emotive men wearing Christian apparel (a shirt with either a Christian slogan such as "His Pain – Your Gain" or "PK: Men of Integrity"), sandals or tennis shoes, and often a baseball cap. As usual, it was a well-mannered, polite, and sincere group. Their Christian sincerity was evidenced by the fact that often the men standing in line to use the porto-potties would still accept the hail from the Jumbotron to bend a knee or prostrate themselves in prayer. The heat and general lack of sleep did not seem to weaken the crowd's resolve.

I would often find my way to the periphery of the crowd where it was easier to talk to individuals. The men would exit the crowd on the mall and stand in the shade and listen to the program. The lack of congestion made it easier to approach people and I would strike up conversations with the men. One such conversation was with Richard Jackson, a trained pastor from Phoenix, AZ, while we were seated on a street curb.

Richard said he attends a Vineyard Christian Fellowship church in Phoenix and has been to several Promise Keepers events, including the Atlanta Clergy conference. He began to share his testimony, specifically, what he credits Promise Keepers for doing in his life. Richard described his race as an American hybrid, as parts of many peoples. He told me how he lost his wife and three children in a car accident more than 11 years ago. After the accident, he wandered from job to job, went through a series of failed relationships, became a drug addict, went through rehabilitation, and lost Christ until he found him three years ago at a Promise Keepers stadium event. He has recently fallen in love (since he stopped "praying for a partner and gave it over to the Lord"), found a church, and become involved in the Phoenix area with the Promise Keepers reconciliation task force. Richard said "Reconciliation is not just about races, but also about denominations, spouses, family, and brothers in Christ. It is a concern we all must focus on."

On another occasion I watched two middle-aged men pray with their young boys near the Washington Monument. They were standing in a circle holding hands. The speaker had asked them to pray and confess the "sexual sins that rob us of a complete relationship with Jesus." After several minutes of prayer, the program continued and the individual groups concluded their prayers.

I approached one of the men and we made our introductions. His name was Tom Lee and he was from Muscatine, IA. He said that he and Benjamin, his 14-year-old son, had traveled to the assembly with a bus load of men from several different congregations. Tom said he and Benjamin had been to previous Promise Keepers events. Benjamin had even made a public affirmation of his commitment to and acceptance of Jesus Christ at the Promise Keepers stadium event in Minneapolis.

I asked Tom why he brought Benjamin to the assembly. He said that "Ben wanted to come, for one reason. He actually contributed $50 toward the cost of the bus trip. He didn't have to pay the money, but it was something he was committed to doing. I also wanted him to come so that he could see me share my faith with other Christians – to be part of this event."

While Tom and I had been talking, Ben and his friend Brandon had taken off their shirts and were playing with a frisbee in the sunshine. Ben had a noticeable scar on the left side of his abdomen. Without prompting, Tom began to discuss the scar: "Ben had a kidney transplant several years ago. I donated one of my kidney's to him. I think that is one of the reasons he takes all this (religion, the assembly) to heart."

I asked Tom if I could talk to Ben for a few minutes about his perceptions of the assembly. Tom said it would be allright, but asked if I would mind if he prayed for me first. I said I would not mind. He took my free hand and voiced a brief prayer.

I asked Ben what he thought of the gathering on the mall. He said he was impressed by the size of the crowd: "I didn't know there was this many Christians in America."

I asked Ben what he had learned from the presentations: "I learned that my prayers can be short and that I can pray to God anytime I want to – that prayer isn't just for church." He also said, concerning the vibrancy of the Christian evangelical community in the U.S., that "It is kind of scary that more missionaries come to the U.S. than to any other country in the world."

Toward the end of the assembly, several Promise Keepers speakers took the stage to pray for racial reconciliation. Every racial group in America was represented. Various speakers came forward to confess racial sins and to forgive those who had sinned against them. A white man was followed by a Native American and then an African American, a Latino, an Asian, a messianic Jew; there was even a representative of those with physical handicaps, a deaf man.

This display of Christian political correctness is grounded in Promise Keepers message of reconciliation: All Christians serve one Lord. Anything that works to keep Christians divided, such as racism, is not God's way but the Devil's. According to Promise Keepers, their form of Christian political correctness is not a faddish device to gain support in racially mixed congregations and communities, as some of its' critics have suggested. Rather, racial reconciliation is presented as based on Scripture and therefore the work of God.

As the assembly came to a close, Bill McCartney took the stage. In a frenzied pace of presentation, McCartney rattled off a series of thoughts concerning the day's events and then discussed the future of Promise Keepers. There had been some talk in the crowd that he was going to make a "big" announcement concerning Promise Keepers, and he fulfilled the crowd's expectations.

McCartney said he sees a need for racial reconciliation within the church, but that the men's ministries need the leadership of clergy in order for it to succeed. He said "Pastors have mostly been working with women" in their ministry, and, while that was worthy, it was time for men to become involved.

McCartney said he "wants local clergy to begin meeting to discuss the needs of the community." The pastors are then to return to their congregations and "tell the men the needs of the community." "That is when God is going to move!" he said. But in order for this to happen, "men need pastors to model racial reconciliation."

To foster "a unity of command" between (PK) men's ministries and clergy, McCartney announced that Promise Keepers would be hosting nine one-day conferences in the spring of 1998 titled "Building Mighty Men of God." The conferences would be provided at no cost to all clergy who would attend.

McCartney told the crowd that the nation was floundering because of racism. He called on the men, led by their clergy, to gather on the steps of every State capital at noon of January 1, 2000, and testify to God that "the giant of racism is dead." He challenged the men, over the next 27 months, to work toward the goal of ending racism and to be ready to pronounce the following statements on the steps of their state's capital:

1. 'Yes', we have a vibrant men's ministry in my church.

2. 'Yes', we have vital prayer partnerships.

3. And, 'Yes' we are racially reconciled.

He told the crowd that with racism dead and the church reconciled, the Promise Keepers would then go global – taking their organizational strengths and the word of the Lord to the rest of the world.

McCartney also told the assembly that Promise Keepers would hold 18 stadium events and 19, somewhat smaller, arena conferences. The conferences would be free to all men. The men were encouraged to bring nonbelievers and "fence-sitters" – those who are Christian, but unconvicted. With the elimination of the $60 conference fee,[15] Promise Keepers is attempting to stanch the decline in conference attendance (notwithstanding the participation at Stand in the Gap) and to broaden the potential support for Promise Keepers. When McCartney finished speaking, he accompanied the assembly in singing the Christian song "I Pledge Allegiance to the Lamb."

As McCartney was speaking, the crowd around me was attentive and intrigued. There was a special sentiment in the crowd concerning McCartney. Some of it arose from curiosity, and some from his penitent charisma. Nonetheless, more than anything else, he is 'the coach.'

There were two men standing immediately in front of me while McCartney was speaking. One was black, the other white. They looked at each other after

McCartney's declaration of Promise Keepers global project and one said "He's got a vision," while the other hooted "Is he a coach or what!"

## Bus Trip Home

It took several hours for all the men to make their way back to RFK stadium to begin our 15-hour return trip to northwest Indiana. Several of the men were late. Three men from the bus formed a circle, held hands, and began to pray for the absent men's safety and for their quick return to the bus. It had been almost three hours since the assembly had ended, and by 9:00 pm everyone had made their way to the bus and we began the all-night journey home.

The time on the bus passed with quiet conversations based on people's reflections. After awhile, Steve put some Promise Keepers video tapes into the bus's video system. The bus was equipped with six small-screen televisions placed at strategic locations. After a Promise Keepers video, and a stop again in Breezewood, PA, the popular movie *Liar, Liar*, starring Jim Carrey was placed in the player. After the movie and another Promise Keepers video, everyone attempted to get some sleep.

In the morning, after we had entered Indiana and everyone had sneaked a few hours of uncomfortable sleep, Steve offered the bus microphone to anyone who wanted to share their thoughts on the assembly. After a pause of approximately one minute without any volunteers, Jim, the convicted motivator, took the microphone. He expressed disappointment in the men for not immediately coming forward to share their testimony with everyone. Jim then gave a brief testimony about the importance of God in his marriage, but his main mission was to encourage others to come forward. And they did.

Bob, the person who organized the communion service the day before, took the microphone. While we had waited for the men to return the night before, Bob and I had time for a conversation. When I asked Bob about the assembly, tears began to form in his eyes and it was difficult for him to maintain his composure.

The night before, Bob had told me that when he looked in his Bible on the bus ride to D.C., he had found an envelope from his wife. He said he knew what it was, but that he did not want to open it until he got to the mall. Once on the mall, he opened his Bible, took out and opened the envelope, and read the letter from his wife. The letter was his wife's way of letting him know how much she and their children loved him. She was proud of what he was doing at the assembly, praised his humility, and said that she loved him for the husband, father, and friend he was to his family. She included pictures of the children in the envelope. Bob said he used the pictures at the assembly; the men were asked to prostrate themselves on the mall while holding pictures of loved ones in their hands during one prayer sequence.

Bob told the bus load of men about the letter and the pictures, all the while fighting back his emotions. He also said he has been clear of his addiction for three years, four months, and 27 days. He did not say what kind of addiction it was; no one seemed less interested for not knowing. He finished his testimony by saying he "hopes God gives him the strength to do more for his wife and children, to enjoy them more, to love them as the Lord loves him."

More than 25 men followed Bob to the front of the bus to share their testimony and reflections on God and the assembly. What follows is a selection of more than an hour and a half of testimony given on the bus.

Bill said he was convicted, point by point, speaker by speaker, while on the mall. He said he really felt the presence of the Holy Spirit while the men were gathered. He said "God got my attention today. We all know God's standard, but too often I'm in the second chair." The "second chair" was a reference to Bob Wilkinson's presentation on the Promise Keepers tape that was played during the evening. A man in the second chair is a Christian who compromises his beliefs in the face of cultural influences and temptations. The individual in the second chair is not 'sold out' for Christ.

A black man took the microphone, telling everyone "it was a pleasure to be among so many godly men attempting to live a clean life." He said "As men, we need to take our rightful place as the head of the home and begin doing what is right for our families." He went on to say that racial reconciliation is tough for men, both black and white, but that God set the rules. "Can we love a brother as a brother?" he asked the crowd, with the men responding with an emphatic 'Yes.'

Another speaker, Ethan, said he was reminded of the story in Joshua about the sin of Achan (Joshua 7). In the story, the Israelites lose a military victory at Ai because Achan is withholding plunder from God. Achan eventually confesses, is stoned to death with his family, and God's favor returns to the Israelites.

Ethan related the story to sin in contemporary society. He said "Your sins affect your family, church and community. It affects us all. If you think your one sin is not affecting others, than you're wrong. Our personal sin affects the nation. Sin is a daily battle we have to take seriously." He concluded by saying "We are going to live, to stand in the gap with God. Hopefully, God will spare this country."

Another Promise Keeper, Alvin, told the men that five years ago he was throwing his life away. He has been to three Promise Keepers events, and he now is convicted in his relationship with Jesus. He has witnessed the benefits. "Five years ago my wife didn't know she was loved; now she knows, and my children know." He went on to say "Love God with your heart, soul, and mind. Now my life can't get any better. Remember to tell the people you love that you love them. Be sure to pray with your wife."

Another man, who introduced himself as 'Pinky,' said the whole weekend had been a pleasure. He gave God the credit for the weather – no clouds, blue sky, and plenty of sunshine. "As I was laying on the ground looking at my daughter's picture I thought to myself that to accomplish anything, God must be at the head of our lives'." Pinky, a social worker, told the men he had rededicated his life to Christ.

Ron credited Promise Keepers and a Marriage Encounter weekend with saving his marriage and family. Ron has been to seven or eight Promise Keepers events. He thanked the group for sharing this time with him and for everyone's blessing. He also thanked his "black brothers for accepting me and for forgiving me." Ron said he was disappointed in the group for watching (and enjoying) the movie *Liar, Liar* because it makes fun of "'straight' people; people who tell the truth." He challenged the men to "go out and live what you have learned this weekend. Go Worship with a brother; go to a black, Latino, or Chinese church. Get involved in the community."

There was also a pair of brothers on the trip, Mike and Pat. Mike spoke first, followed by Pat. Mike told the audience that "Year after year I get disgusted with myself for slipping up in life. I want to encourage you that the walk with Christ is a process. Our God is a God of many chances – it's not easy, but we follow Jesus to the cross."

Mike also had some advice for the single men on the bus, specifically his brother Pat. He told the single men to "Ask the Lord for a woman who is radical – radical for Christ – someone who sits in the 'first chair' (someone sold out for Christ). Be sure to look in the right places, such as church groups or other religious gatherings."

Pat took the microphone from Mike, with Mike kneeling in the aisle approximately three feet from his brother. He knew his brother well enough to know that if he was going to speak in public, he must have something weighing on his heart.

Pat began by saying he was lucky to be with the group because he had "hit rock bottom years ago." Pat had been through a terrible divorce, ending a marriage in which he had thought he had married his best friend only to see it fall apart in less than four years. He told the men how he had come from a "broken family." He shared how his dad had always asked him "Why can't you be like Mike?"

At this point, tears slowly rolling down his face, Pat and Mike embraced. Pat finished his testimony by thanking Mike and Promise Keepers for bringing Christ into his life. Mike and Pat walked to the back of bus to hearty handshakes and slaps on the back.

Steve, the trip organizer, closed the session, by telling the men "A man who can share his pain with strangers is a man who can walk with Christ."

## Concluding Thought

Steve's closing words reminded me of something out of Nietzsche's critique of Christianity, only with admiration rather than contempt. Or maybe it was closer to Zarathustra's discussion with the higher men.

In Zarathustra's cave overlooking a world of abysses, one of the higher men, the magician, describes how they "are suffering of *the great nausea*, for whom the old god has died and for whom no new god lies as yet in cradles and swaddling clothes . . . ."[16] Languishing in nausea, they look to Zarathustra for "the way" (which does not exist, according to Zarathustra) and vitalism – for something in a cradle and swaddling clothes.

By the fourth and last part of Nietzsche's work, Zarathustra has overcome his nausea, but another hurdle lingers. Previous to the gathering in the cave, the soothsayer, the proclaimer of great weariness ("all is the same, nothing is worth while, the world is without meaning, knowledge strangles"[17]), comes to Zarathustra and asks if he has heard it yet, the cry of distress from man, and in particular, the higher men. The soothsayer tells Zarathustra that he has come to seduce him to his final sin, that greatest of dangers, the sin of pity.

Nausea and pity are mitigating effects to those who attempt to study the values and relationships of others. As feelings, they mingle with anger, disgust, love, sorrow, and spite to form contradicting and compelling emotional states. I struggled with nausea and pity while researching the Promise Keepers. They would barge into my consciousness at that so-called line between participant and nonparticipant observer. The nausea was easier to dispel than the pity, since even the convalescent can find value in what has stricken him. But pity bleeds into the senses of observing and listening; it is what one risks in the invitation to seek the other.

One cannot spend extensive time with Promise Keepers (or any group) without witnessing the wounds of life, the discomforts, anxieties, and burdens of the camel. The men have experienced pain, some more than others, but not unlike the pain anyone may experience; in other words, their pain is not unique. They too are cast to the sea of humanity, but they are not outcasts since they are captured by a particular fisherman.[18]

There is pity among and between the Promise Keepers, but little pitying. They do not *feel pity for* each other. 'To feel pity for' is a hail imposed on and/or accepted by the witness, an interpellation of sorrow with a disposition to help. There is little of this among Promise Keepers.

In the Promise Keepers ideological practice, pity is experienced as empathy. Each PK understands, to varying degrees, the trials and tribulations of walking to the cross with Christ. They empathize with Pat's failed marriage, Bob's struggle with addiction, and a man's confessed ignorance of racism. They are there for their brothers with hugs, a shoulder to cry on, and hands to hold in prayer, but the Lord takes care of the rest. To pity (the disposition to help) is a burden carried by the Lord and not the individual Promise Keeper. It is the Promise Keeper's responsibility to have Christ-like empathy, but not to pity; empathy bonds the men together, whereas pitying attempts to alleviate the misfortune of another. The walk with Christ is something to share with men, even strangers, but the pain, the interpellation of pitying, is given over to the Lord.

## Notes

1. See Christopher Hitchens, "Another March, Another Prick in the Wall," *The Nation* (October 27, 1997), 9.

2. Promise Keepers Stand in the Gap Brochure (1997), 5.

3. See also the *Stand in the Gap: A Sacred Assembly of Men* program. On page 4 in an answer to "What is a Sacred Assembly?" the program lists a shortened version of 2 Timothy 3:1-5, stating: "But mark this; There will be terrible times in the last days. People will be lovers of themselves, lovers of money, boastful, proud, abusive, disobedient to their parents, ungrateful, unholy, without love . . . lovers of pleasure rather than lovers of God – having a form of godliness, but denying its power."

4. For a critique of media coverage and the "silence of liberal organizations" concerning Promise Keepers Sacred Assembly see Katha Pollitt, "The Promised Land," *The Nation* (October 27, 1997), 10.

5. NOW Homepage, now.org (September 1997).

6. Raleigh Washington, Glen Kehrein, and Claude V. King, *Break Down the Walls: Experiencing Biblical Reconciliation and Unity in the Body of Christ* (Chicago: Moody Press, 1997).

7. Joe Maxwell, "'Til Race Do Us Part?" *New Man* (January-February 1997), 26-31.

8. A similar critique to NOW's is offered by Michael Kimmel, "Promise Keepers: Patriarchy's Second Coming as Masculine Renewal," in *TIKKUN*, Vol. 12, No. 2 (1996), 46-50. Kimmel discusses PK's program of racial reconciliation in the following manner: "Theirs is not a call to support those programs that would uplift the race and set the nation on a course toward racial equality. This is not about anti-discrimination legislation or affirmative action – heck, it's not even about integration. It's about being kinder and more civil. It's about hearing their pain, not supporting its alleviation. It's choosing to be nicer, but not about policies that force us to be fairer. In the PK world view, racial reconciliation is an individual posture, but not a collective struggle." (49)

9. NOW Homepage, now.org (September 1997).

10. Wagner, "Strong Mentoring Relationships," in *Seven Promises of a Promise Keeper,* ed. Al Janssen (Colorado Springs: Focus on the Family Publishing, 1994), 59. See also Gary Smalley, "Five Secrets of a Happy Marriage," in *Seven Promises of a Promise Keeper,* ed. Al Janssen (Colorado Springs: Focus on the Family Publishing, 1994), 105-113; Dr. James C. Dobson, "The Priority of Fathering," in *Seven Promises of a Promise Keeper,* ed. Al Janssen (Colorado Springs: Focus on the Family Publishing, 1994), 115-127; Dennis Rainey, "Putting Aside Your Pride," in *What Makes a Man?,* ed. Stephen Griffith (Colorado Springs: NavPress, 1992), 78-79; Steve Farrar, "Real Men Don't," in *What Makes a Man?,* ed. Stephen Griffith (Colorado Springs: NavPress, 1992), 80-81.

11. Dr. Tony Evans, "Spiritual Purity," in *Seven Promises of a Promise Keeper,* ed. Al Janssen (Colorado Springs: Focus on the Family Publishing, 1994), 79.

12. Ibid., 76-79; According to Evans, see Job 29.

13. Promise Keepers News Homepage, promisekeepers.org (October 1997).

14. Ibid.

15. Promise Keepers have been requesting donations to offset the loss of support from ticket sales. According to an account by Steve Kloehn reported in the *Chicago Tribune* on 6 October 1997, it may already be working. Kloehn reports "overflowing trash barrels used to collect donations" at the D.C. rally.

16. Friedrich Nietzsche, *Thus Spoke Zarathustra: A Book for None and All*, trans. Walter Kaufmann (New York: Penguin Books, 1978), 297. (Italics in original.)

17. Ibid., 241.

18. See Nietzsche, *Thus Spoke Zarathustra*: "For if the world is like a dark jungle and a garden of delight for all wild hunters, it strikes me even more, and so I prefer to think of it, as an abysmal, rich sea – a sea full of colorful fish and crabs, which even gods might covet, that for their sakes they would wish to become fisherman and net-throwers; so rich is the world in queer things, great and small. Especially the human world, the human sea: *that* is where I now cast my golden fishing rod and say: Open up, you human abyss!" (238)

# Chapter Six

---

## Mere Thoughts

People are always asking me, "So, what do you think of the Promise Keepers?" I suppose it is an obvious question once they find out I have been reading about, meeting with, and observing the Promise Keepers for more than three years. But answering or even beginning to address the question is very difficult. What do 'I' think of the Promise Keepers? Well, that depends.

It is fashionable to say that knowledge depends on your perspective. This is true and yet somewhat misleading. It is true that one's world is experienced through a fairly limited range of perspectives, and with limitation comes a narrowing of knowledge. But it is also partly a falsification to say knowledge is determined by one's perspective, perhaps because it seems too simplistic, self-comforting, and religious, that is, faith based.

But, I am not sure I believe that either. Nonetheless, in the final analysis, questions about how knowledge is acquired are of little concern to the Promise Keepers. Perspective is important to them, but it is a first order perspective they rely on; the world has a basic reality, which can be known through the bible and the love of Jesus Christ. Baudrillard's second, third, and fourth orders of reality are all false perspectives to them, perspectives held by not-yet-believers.[1] With a first order perspective, better known as the truth, the Promise Keepers exclude themselves from an aleatory journey toward knowledge and a democratic, that is, unruly, discussion of truth. Democratic societies have truth statements (all men, no, now it is all people are created equal), but they are malleable, depending on contending values. The PK truth perspective still must be interpreted, but it eliminates much discussion. On the other hand, perhaps first order perspectives are less malignant than others.

So, what do I think of the Promise Keepers? I do not know. At times they were very compelling, and dare I say, seductive. They were kind, honest, sincere, and friendly. They never refused my queries or attempted to exclude me from their conversations. They were willing to share their most personal experiences, the humiliating and the august, without hesitation, usually without my even asking. Nothing was ever 'off the record'; their stories were given to me as gifts. Their willingness to share (witness) is fundamental to their humility and is cultivated in and through their faith in Christ.

I also found them to be pathetic, weak, tormented, and pained. How is that possible you might ask? We differ on metaphysical principles, I suppose. I would often see a Promise Keeper as a bewildered other – a victim – a slave – a weak man in need of comfort and direction, in need of a concierge. The interesting point is that they embrace these characterizations. They recognize they are victims of Adam's sin, slaves to this world, and weak men in need of the loving grace of Jesus. These "negative" characterizations are espoused as signs of strength, as God's will.

Bound to or constitutive of one's perspective are the values held within a perspective. A perspective is not a vacuous island where one then entertains the world that abounds. Rather, each perspective is always already laced with values; laced as in tied up and also poisoned, contaminated, or tainted. Every perspective maintains a form of depth and weight, even the schizo's perspective; if not, weightlessness is disabling and one floats, without tension, in a distensed plateau.

Something good about Promise Keepers? Sure, why not. For example, a father taking his son to breakfast on a Saturday morning. The father sat happily in the booth coloring with his son. The boy, approximately eight years old, found it hard to eat his pancakes what with coloring, telling his father about his week, and dreamily allowing his stuffed animal a sip out of his glass of chocolate milk. After a leisurely meal, the two left the restaurant holding hands, both smiling as they walked into the humid summer morning.

Something bad about Promise Keepers? Sure, again, why not. For example, the Bible as literal truth, the reliance/acceptance of a moral order based on original sin, which happens to be caused by a woman, or the convenience of a masculine holy trinity.

Judgements of Good and Bad. What a strangely familiar place to end this fare (archaic; journey and also one's diet). Is not that the place this sort of text has to be delivered?

## Note

1. Jean Baudrillard, *Simulations*, trans. by Paul Foss, Paul Patton and Philip Beitchman (New York: Semiotext(e)). A first order of reality is when the image "is the reflection of a basic reality." In second, third, and fourth orders of reality the image "masks and perverts a basic reality"; "masks the absence of a basic reality"; "bears no relation to any reality whatever: it is its own pure simulacrum."(11)

# Appendix

THE SEVEN PROMISES OF A PROMISE KEEPER

1. A Promise Keeper is committed to honor Jesus Christ through worship, prayer, and obedience to His Word in the power of the Holy Spirit.

2. A Promise Keeper is committed to pursue vital relationships with a few other men, understanding that he needs his brothers to help keep his promises.

3. A Promise Keeper is committed to practice spiritual, moral, ethical, and sexual purity.

4. A Promise Keeper is committed to build strong marriages and families through love, protection, and Biblical values.

5. A Promise Keeper is committed to support the mission of the church, by honoring and praying for his pastor and by actively giving his time and resources.

6. A Promise Keeper is committed to reach beyond any racial and denominational barriers to demonstrate the power of Biblical unity.

7. A Promise Keeper is committed to influence his world, being obedient to the Great Commandment (Mark 12:30-31) (love the Lord) and the Great Commission (make disciples of all nations, teaching them the Lord's way) (Matthew 28:19-20).

# Bibliography

Abraham, Ken. "God Loves Losers, Too!" In *What Makes A Man?* Edited by Stephen Griffith. Colorado Springs: NavPress, 1992.

____. "Acceptance at What Price?" In *What Makes A Man?* Edited by Stephen Griffith. Colorado Springs: NavPress, 1992.

____. "Traveler's Advisory." In *What Makes A Man?* Edited by Stephen Griffith. Colorado Springs: NavPress, 1992.

____. *Who Are the Promise Keepers?: Understanding the Christian Men's Movement*. New York: Doubleday, 1997.

Althusser, Louis. *Lenin and Philosophy and Other Essays*. Translated by Ben Brewster. New York: Monthly Review Press, 1971.

Arms, Phil. *Promise Keepers: Another Trojan Horse*. Houston, TX: Shiloh Publishers, 1997.

Bataille, Georges. *Theory of Religion*. New York: Zone Books, 1994.

Baudrillard, Jean. *Simulations*. Translated by Paul Foss, Paul Patton, and Philip Beitchman. New York: Semiotext(e), 1983.

____. *Symbolic Exchange and Death*. Translated by Iain Hamilton Gain. Thousand Oaks, CA: Sage Publications, 1995.

Beauvoir, Simone de. *The Second Sex*. Reprint. New York: Vintage Books, 1989.

Bebbington, David W. "Evangelicalism in Its Settings: The British and American Movements Since 1940." In *Evangelicalism: Comparative Studies of Popular Protestantism in North America, British Isles, and Beyond, 1700-1990*. Edited by Mark A. Noll, David W. Bebbington, and George A. Rawlyk. Oxford: Oxford University Press, 1994.

Bellah, Robert N., Richard Madsen, William M. Sullivan, Ann Swidler, and Steven M. Tipton. *Habits of the Heart: Individualism and Commitment in American Life*. Berkeley: University of California Press, 1985.

Bellant, Russ. "Mania in the Stadia: The Origins and Goals of Promise Keepers." *Front Lines Research*, May 1995.

Bendroth, Margaret Lamberts. *Fundamentalism & Gender, 1875 to the Present*. New Haven, CT: Yale University Press, 1993.

Bernotsky, R. Lorraine, and Joan M. Bernotsky. "Promise Keepers: Politics and Religion in a Contemporary Men's Movement." Paper Presented at the *American Political Science Association*, August 1997.

Black, Jim Nelson. "The Heart of the New Man." *New Man*, November/December 1994.

Bly, Robert. *Iron John: A Book About Men.* Reading, MA: Addison-Wesley Publishing, 1990.

Bouey, Debra. "James Ryle's Vineyard Theology." Reprint. *The Christian Conscience*, February 1996.

Bright, Bill. *The Coming Revival: America's Call To Fast, Pray and "Seek God's Face."* Orlando, FL: New Life Publications, 1995.

Bruns, Roger A. *Preacher: Billy Sunday & Big Time American Evangelism.* New York: WW Norton, 1992.

Burke, Kip. "Promise Keepers Calls Men to 'Stand in the Gap.'" *New Man*, March/April 1997.

Butler, Judith. *Gender Trouble: Feminism and the Subversion of Identity.* New York: Routledge, 1990.

____. *Bodies That Matter: On the Discursive Limits of "Sex."* New York: Routledge, 1993.

Ciznik, Richard. "The State of the Union." *Charisma*, January 1996.

Clarkson, Frederick. "Righteous Brothers." *In These Times*, August 5, 1996.

Clatterbaugh, Kenneth. *Contemporary Perspectives on Masculinity: Men, Women, and Politics in Modern Society,* 2nd ed. Boulder, CO: Westview Press, 1997.

Cloud, David W. "Beware of Promise Keepers." Reprint. *O Timothy Magazine* 11, no. 6, 1994.

Coleman, James S. "Social Capital in the Creation of Human Capital." *American Journal of Sociology* 94, Supplement S95-S120, 1988.

Colson, Charles W., with Nancy R. Pearcey. *A Dance With Deception: Revealing the Truth Behind the Headline*. Dallas: Word Publishing, 1993.

Colson, Charles W. "A Man and His Integrity." In *Go the Distance.* Edited by John Trent. Colorado Springs: Focus on the Family Publishing, 1996.

Conason, Joe, Alfred Ross, and Lee Cokorinos. "The Promise Keepers are Coming: The Third Wave of the Religious Right." *The Nation*, October 7, 1996.

Cooper, Rodney L. *Double Bind: Escaping the Contradictory Demands of Manhood.* Grand Rapids, MI: Zondervan Publishing House, 1996.

Crabb, Larry. "Masculinity." In *What Makes a Man?* Edited by Stephen Griffith. Colorado Springs: NavPress, 1992.

Derrida, Jacques. *The Ear of the Other: Otobiography, Transference, Translation.* Translated by Peggy Kamuf. Lincoln, NE: University of Nebraska Press, 1988.

Dobson, James C., Dr. "The Priority of Fathering." In *Seven Promises of a Promise Keeper.* Edited by Al Janssen and Larry K. Weeden. Colorado Springs: Focus on the Family Publishing, 1994.

Ellis, William T., LL.D. *"Billy" Sunday: The Man and His Message.* Philadelphia: John C. Winston, 1914.

Evans, Tony, Dr. "Spiritual Purity." In *Seven Promises of a Promise Keeper.* Edited by Al Janssen and Larry K. Weeden. Colorado Springs: Focus on the Family Publishing, 1994.

Fackre, Gabriel. *Ecumenical Faith in Evangelical Perspective.* Grand Rapids, MI: William B. Eerdmans Publishing, 1993.

Farrar, Steve. "Real Men Don't." In *What Makes a Man?* Edited by Stephen Griffith. Colorado Springs: NavPress Publishing, 1992.

Foucault, Michel. *The Archaeology of Knowledge & The Discourse on Language.* Translated by A.M. Sheridan Smith. New York: Pantheon Books, 1972.

Fowler, Robert Booth, and Allen D. Hertzke. *Religion and Politics in America: Faith, Culture, and Strategic Choices.* Boulder, CO: Westview Press, 1995.

Frame, Randy. "Is Christ or Satan Ruler of This World?" *Christianity Today,* March 5, 1990.

____. "Plan Calls for Doing Away with Public Schools, IRS." *Christianity Today,* November 19, 1990.

Goeringer, Conrad F. "Godly Men with a Dominionist Agenda." *American Atheist,* Spring 1997.

Goldberg, Herbert. *The New Male: From Self-Destruction to Self-Care.* New York: William Morrow, 1979.

Gorsuch, Geoff, with Dan Schaffer. *BROTHERS! Calling Men Into Vital Relationships: A Small Group Discussion Guide.* Colorado Springs: NavPress, 1994.

Hagopian, David, and Douglas Wilson. *Beyond Promises: A Biblical Challenge to Promise Keepers.* Moscow, ID: Canon Press, 1996.

Hayford, Jack. "Though I Speak In Tongues." *Charisma,* March 1993.

Hicks, Robert. *Uneasy Manhood.* Nashville: Oliver-Nelson, 1991.

____. "Why Men Feel So Out of Place at Church." In *What Makes a Man?* Edited by Stephen Griffith. Colorado Springs: NavPress, 1992.

____. "Why Beer Commercials Make Some Men Feel So Good." In *What Makes a Man?* Edited by Stephen Griffith. Colorado Springs: NavPress, 1992.

____. *The Masculine Journey: The Six Stages of Manhood.* Colorado Springs: NavPress, 1993.

Hicks, Robert, and Dietrich Gruen. *The Masculine Journey: A Promise Keepers Study Guide.* Colorado Springs: NavPress, 1993.

Hitchens, Christopher. "Another March, Another Prick in the Wall." *The Nation,* October 27, 1997.

Horner, Bob, Ron Ralston, and David Sunde. *Promise Builders Study Series: Applying the Seven Promises.* Colorado Springs: Focus on the Family Publishing, 1996.

____. *Promise Builders Study Series: The Promise Keeper At Work.* Colorado Springs: Focus on the Family Publishing, 1996.

Ireland, Patricia. "A Look At . . . Promise Keepers: Beware of 'Feel-Good Male Supremacy.'" *Washington Post*, September 7, 1997.

Janssen, Al and Larry K. Weeden. Editors. *Seven Promises of a Promise Keeper*. Colorado Springs: Focus on the Family Publishing, 1994.

Kimbrell, Andrew. *The Masculine Mystique: The Politics of Masculinity.* New York: Ballantine Books, 1995.

Kimmel, Michael S. *Manhood in America: A Cultural History.* New York: The Free Press, 1996.

____. "Promise Keepers: Patriarchy's Second Coming as Masculine Renewal." *TIKKUN* 12, no. 2, February 1996.

Kloehn, Steve. "Promise Keepers task: Don't lose momentum." *Chicago Tribune*, October 6, 1997.

Lacan, Jacques. *Feminine Sexuality.* Edited by Juliet Mitchell and Jacqueline Rose. Translated by Jacqueline Rose. New York: W.W. Norton, 1985.

Leslie, Lynn and Sarah Leslie. "The New Gnostics: Resurrecting Pagan Rites – Part 3." Reprint. *The Christian Conscience,* February 1996.

Lewis, Gregg. *The Power of a Promise Kept: Life Stories by Gregg Lewis.* Colorado Springs: Focus on the Family Publishing, 1995.

Lobel, Kerry. *National Gay and Lesbian Task Force Press Statement: Promise Keepers*, June 13, 1997.

MacKinnon, Catharine A. *Toward a Feminist Theory of the State*. Cambridge, MA: Harvard University Press, 1989.

Mannheim, Karl. *Ideology and Utopia: An Introduction to the Sociology_of Knowledge*. Translated by Louis Wirth and Edward Shils. New York: A Harvest Book, 1985.

Mathews, Jane De Hart. "The New Feminism and the Dynamics of Social Change." In *Women's America: Refocusing the Past.* Edited by Linda K. Kerber and Jane De Hart Mathews. New York: Oxford University Press, 1982.

Maxwell, Joe. "'Til Race Do Us Part?" *New Man,* January/February 1997.

McCartney, Bill. "It's Time for Men to Take a Stand." In *What Makes a Man?* Edited by Stephen Griffith. Colorado Springs: NavPress Publishing Group, 1992.

____. "Seeking God's Favor." In *Seven Promises of a Promise Keeper* Edited by Al Janssen and Larry K. Weeden. Colorado Springs: Focus on the Family Publishing, 1994.

____. "God Is Calling Us to a Higher Love." In *Go The Distance: The Making of a Promise Keeper.* Edited by John Trent. Colorado Springs: Focus on the Family Publishing, 1996.

____. *Stand In The Gap: The Prayer Journal.* Dallas: Word Publishing, 1997.

____. Letter to conference attendees. Promise Keepers Homepage, 1997.

____. "Promise Makers." *Policy Review*, September-October, 1997.

McCartney, Bill, with Dave Diles. *From Ashes to Glory*. Nashville: Thomas Nelson Publishers, 1995.

McCartney, Bill, with David Halbrook. *Sold Out: Becoming Man Enough to Make a Difference*. Nashville: Word Publishing, 1997.

McIntyre, Alasdair. *After Virtue*. South Bend, IN: University of Notre Dame Press, 1981.

Messner, Michael A. *Politics of Masculinities: Men in Movements*. Thousand Oaks: Sage Publications, 1997.

Neiberger, Ami. "Promise Keepers: Seven Reasons to Watch Out." Reprint. *Freedom Writer* (Institute for First Amendment Studies), September 1996.

Nietzsche, Friedrich. *Ecce Homo: How one becomes what one is*. From the complete works of F. Nietzsche, volume 17. Translated by Anthony M. Ludovici. Edinburgh: Morrison and Gibb Limited, 1911.

____. *Thus Spoke Zarathustra: A Book for None and All*. Translated by Walter Kaufmann. New York: Penguin Books, 1978.

____. *The Birth of Tragedy and The Genealogy of Morals*. Translated by Francis Golffing. New York: Anchor Books, Doubleday, 1990.

____. *Beyond Good and Evil*. Translated by R.J. Hollingdale. New York: Penguin Books, 1990.

Nisbet, Robert A. *Community and Power (formerly The Quest for Community)*. New York: A Galaxy Book, 1962.

Oliver, Gary J. "Black-and-White Living in a Gray World." In *Seven Promises of A Promise Keeper*. Edited by Al Jannsen and Larry K. Weeden. Colorado Springs: Focus on the Family Publishing, 1994.

Palms, Roger. "A Man's Fixed Reference." In *What Makes a Man?* Edited by Stephen Griffith. Colorado Springs: NavPress, 1992.

Phillips, Randy. "Foreword." In *Go The Distance: The Making of a Promise Keeper*. Edited by John Trent. Colorado Springs: Focus on the Family Publishing, 1996.

Pollitt, Katha. "The Promised Land." In *The Nation*, October 27, 1997.

Promise Keepers Conference Information Packet. 1996.

Promise Keepers Ambassador Pamphlet. 1996.

Promise Keepers Ambassador Training Level One. 1995.

Promise Keepers New Testament Bible (NIV). *Man of His Word*. Colorado Springs: International Bible Society, 1996.

Promise Keepers Men's Conference Brochure. *The Making of a Godly Man*. 1997.

Promise Keepers Conference Program. 1996.

Promise Keepers Statement of Faith. 1995.

Putnam, Robert D. "The Prosperous Community: Social Capital and Public Life." *The American Prospect* 13, 1993.

____. "Bowling Alone: America's Declining Social Capital." *Journal of Democracy* 6, no. 1, 1995.

____. "Tuning In, Tuning Out: The Strange Disappearance of Social Capital in America." *PS: Political Science & Politics*, December 1995.

Raab, Scott. "Triumph of His Will." *GQ*, January 1996.

Rainey, Dennis. "Putting Aside Your Pride." In *What Makes a Man?* Edited by Stephen Griffith. Colorado Springs: NavPress, 1992.

Richardson, Pete. *Focusing Your Men's Ministry: A Strategy for Layleaders and Pastors*. Boulder, CO: Promise Keepers, 1993.

Riley, William Bell. *Wives of the Bible: A Cross-Section of Femininity.* Grand Rapids, MI: Zondervan, 1938.

Rosin, Hanna. "Promise Weepers; The Right embraces sentimentality." *New Republic*, October 27, 1997.

Rousseau, Jean-Jacques. *Politics and the Arts: Letter to M. D'Alembert on the Theatre*. Translated by Allan Bloom. Glencoe, IL: The Free Press, 1960.

Rowbotham, Sheila. *Woman's Consciousness, Man's World.* Harmondsworth: Penguin, 1973.

Ryle, James. *Hippo in the Garden: A Non Religious Approach to having a Conversation with God.* Orlando, FL: Creation House, 1993.

____. *A Dream Come True*. Orlando, FL: Creation House, 1995.

Schwalbe, Michael. *Unlocking the Iron Cage: The Men's Movement, Gender Politics, and American Culture.* New York: Oxford University Press, 1996.

Scott, Joan W. "Experience." In *Feminists Theorize The Political.* Edited by Judith Butler and Joan W. Scott. New York: Routledge, 1992.

Smalley, Gary and John Trent. "The Promises You Make to Yourself." In *What Makes a Man?* Edited by Stephen Griffith. Colorado Springs: NavPress, 1992.

____. "The Promises You Make to Your Wife." In *What Makes a Man?* Edited by Stephen Griffith. Colorado Springs: NavPress, 1992.

____. "The Promises You Make to Your Family." In *What Makes a Man?* Edited by Stephen Griffith. Colorado Springs: NavPress, 1992.

Smalley, Gary. "Five Secrets of a Happy Marriage." In *Seven Promises of a Promise Keeper.* Edited by Al Janssen and Larry K. Weeden. Colorado Springs: Focus on the Family Publishing, 1994.

Snyder, Howard A. "Will Promise Keepers Keep Their Promises?" *Christianity Today*, November 14, 1994.

Stanley, Charles. "The Sensitive Man and Romance." In *What Makes a Man?* Edited by Stephen Griffith. Colorado Springs: NavPress, 1992.

Sterling Research Associates. *Promise Keepers: The Third Wave of the American Religious Right*, unpublished manuscript. New York: Sterling Research Associates, 1996.

Strode, Tom. "3 SBC Pastors Join Call for GOP to stay Pro-Life." *Baptist Press News,* March 12, 1996.

Swomley, John M. "Storm Troopers in the Culture War." In *The Humanist*, September/October 1997.

Tarkowski, Ed. "Part Two: Foundations For Apostasy: 1986-1996." Unpublished manuscript, 1996.

*The Student Bible: New International Version.* Notes by Philip Yancey and Tim Stafford. Grand Rapids, MI: Zondervan Publishing, 1996.

Thomas, Lee. *The Billy Sunday Story: The Life and Times of William Ashley Sunday, D.D. An authorized biography*. Grand Rapids, MI: Zondervan Publishing, 1961.

Trent, John. *Go The Distance: The Making of a Promise Keeper.* Colorado Springs: Focus on the Family Publishing, 1996.

____. Editor. *The Making of a Godly Man Workbook.* Colorado Springs: Focus on the Family Publishing, 1997.

Wagner, E. Glenn, Ph.D., with Dietrich Gruen. *Strategies For A Successful Marriage: A Study Guide For Men.* Colorado Springs: NavPress, 1994.

Wagner, E. Glenn, Ph.D. 1994. "Strong Mentoring Relationships." In *Seven Promises of a Promise Keeper.* Edited by Al Janssen and Larry K. Weeden. Colorado Springs: Focus on the Family Publishing, 1994.

Wald, Kenneth D. *Religion and Politics in the United States*, third edition. Washington, DC: Congressional Quarterly Press, 1996.

Washington, Raleigh, Glen Kehrein, and Claude V. King. *Break Down the Walls: Experiencing Biblical Reconciliation and Unity in the Body of Christ.* Chicago: Moody Press, 1997.

Weinstein, Deena and Michael A. Weinstein. *Postmodern(ized) Simmel.* New York: Routledge, 1993.

Widrig, Carl, Jr. "Is God Saying What James Ryle is Saying?" Reprint. *The Christian Conscience*, May 1996.

Wilcox, Clyde. *God's Warriors: The Christian Right in Twentieth-Century America.* Baltimore, MD: The Johns Hopkins University Press, 1992.

Zweir, Robert. *Born-Again Politics: The New Christian Right in America.* Downers Grove, IL: InterVarsity Press, 1982.

# Index

## About the Author

Bryan Brickner received his Ph.D. in Political Science from Purdue University in 1997. He is a mosaic artist and freelance writer living in Chicago.